SHIFTING FREQUENCIES

UPLIFT YOUR LIFE
USING
QUANTUM HEALING ACTIVATION TECHNIQUE

ANNETT SCHNEIDER,
Quantum Healing Transformation
CREATOR OF Q.H.A.T.

Copyright © 2019 by Annett Schneider
All rights reserved.

This book or any portion thereof may not be reproduced or used in any manner whatsoever without the express written permission of the publisher except for the use of brief quotations in a book review.

Table Of Contents

PART I: Shifting Frequencies Quantum Healing 1
Testimonials 1
Introduction 3
Chapter 1: Identity Crisis & Quantum Frequency 4
Chapter 2: Transformation Techniques 9

PART II: shifting frequencies through food 12
Chapter 3: Boundaries 16
Chapter 4: Recharging Your Systems, Organs And Chakras 22
Chapter 5: Nurture And Nourish 27

PART III: Shifting Frequencies With Thought 32
Chapter 6: Taming The Mind 36
Chapter 7: Mighty I AM Presence 40
Chapter 8: You Are The Filter 45
Chapter 9: Divine Knowledge 50
Chapter 10: The Power of Imagination 55
Chapter 11: Being Your Authentic Self 60
Chapter 12: The Source Of All That Is 72
Chapter 13: Being Mentally Responsible 80
About The Author 93

Testimonials

SPINE STRAIGHTENED, PAIN RELIEVED

After having quantum healing, my body was realigned from the base of my spine to my head. **I can now get out of bed without pain and bend over without pain, which I had my whole life, due to the twist in my spine.** I'm happy to share this healing which has helped me so much! Solandra Elacondra, Calgary, AB

CAT'S ESOPHAGUS CLEARED IN 1 SESSION

My friend's cat wasn't eating and I didn't know why. Annett did quantum healing and she could see there was a block in her esophagus. **The block was dissolved and my cat was able to eat again after that session!** I am so grateful and it saved me a trip to the vet!

SE, Calgary, AB.

SHOULDER PAIN GONE!

During my remote energy healing with Annett, **I could feel the heat in my body and was surprised and so happy when the pain in my shoulders was gone! I could literally feel where she was working in my body, she also balanced my spine** and at the end I felt amazing, lighter, pain relieved and happy! Ron., Surrey, BC

PAIN RELEASED, SINUSES & LYMPHATIC CLEARED!

My whole life has changed since our session in ways I couldn't imagine! **My arm and shoulder pain is gone. Heaviness is lifted and I feel joy! I finally feel love again for my Mom instead of resentment that was trapped in my lymphatic system and released! My neck pain (for years) was gone in minutes. I could feel the healing in my foot during the session and my head pain is almost gone. **My sinuses cleared by 95% during the session**. I am amazed, this is a huge change for me. -Cynthia, Oregon

EXTREME BACK PAIN GONE, SINUSES CLEARED!

My remote energy healing with Annett released severe back pain that I was struggling with, it was hard to sit, walk or move without extreme pain. **I could feel where Annett was sending the energy to my body and felt the release and relief. The pain was gone!** She was also able to clear my sinuses which were chronically blocked from surgery scar tissue and I can sleep through the night now, previously I had been waking up several times with breathing problems! Thank you!

L.H. Surrey, BC

SHE CHANGED MY BODY & MY LIFE!

I hurt my neck years ago and had problems ever since. **After my session with Annett I feel better and in less chronic pain than I have in years!! My neck is particularly miraculous! For my back, having tried many times with other methods, it never could be put right and you put the rotate disc back in!! The lump in my chest is gone, I can breathe better and sing better. My jaw moved back into place and the numbness is gone!** Thank you for changing my body and my life. I will be having regular "tune ups" with you. Suzyn, White Rock, BC

INTRODUCTION

This book is a combination of 3 parts. They each represent a different aspect of ourselves that we need to work with in order to fully be ourselves at our highest level.

The first part is how to heal ourselves with energy that is beyond 3D or "quantum". Learning to work with the sacred heart or heart frequency, to shift the consciousness of the body so it can heal itself.

The second part is about the physical body, addiction, and how to heal chronic illness in whatever form it takes. Quite often it takes the form of sugar addiction which has an emotional root cause. This needs to be cleared in order to be free of it and for the healing to be permanent.

The third part are messages transmitted from the Master Kuthumi and messages from Annett's spirit guides who shares powerful wisdom on how to use the power of your mind in a constructive way rather than destructive.

Connecting with the three aspects of energy, body and wisdom you can transform your life and recreate yourself.

◆ CHAPTER 1 ◆

IDENTITY CRISIS & QUANTUM FREQUENCY

Do you feel like you're going through an identity crisis? Everyone on some level is going through this on the Earth right now. With all of the upheaval and changes happening it's hard to know which end is up.

This book is for those of you who are seeking transformation. It feels like your old reality is complete and you're not quite sure where you're going next. It's hard to "die" sometimes; that's what it takes to get to the next level. A death of the old self, old reality and who you think you are, or need to be.

Sometimes we need to be in between realities. This can be a very uncomfortable place to be. The old reality is gone and the new hasn't quite shown up yet. The new can't be created until the slate is clean. So if you find yourself in a very uncomfortable place emotionally, physically and feels as if your very foundation is being ripped away, the slate is being cleaned.

If you have crutches you have been using, such as relationships, addictions, or a job that no longer supports who you are, they will become unbearable to hold onto.

Why not take that leap and let go so the new reality can start to show up?

The path will be shown if you take a step in the direction that feels best to you. Not just what you think you should do or making a decision based on fear, but what resonates with you.

I'm recreating my life based on what feels good for me. My connection to quantum energy and using the frequency of the heart has shown me shifts in the body and emotions I didn't know was possible.

When running this frequency for myself and others, a connection is made where there wasn't one before. It goes beyond third dimensional senses and I see, feel and hear inside the body of humans or animals. As the frequency runs through my spiritual heart center to them, their system begins to move into alignment, balance and heal itself. As I tune into each organ or system I can sense what is going on with it, see if there are emotional or physical blocks and connect to the consciousness of each body part. Quantum healing removes the energy imprint in the cell that's causing the imbalance and supports the body in healing itself.

When I'm in a quiet space, I start running heart frequency to my body. It's a powerful tool to heal myself. I begin by focusing my attention on my upper chest, sacred or spiritual heart centre and send energy to my organs or systems. As I connect to that part of my body, I begin to feel very relaxed, feel healing energy flowing, feel changes such as pain relief (sometimes pain increase as it heals) and sometimes emotional release. I feel a connection to my body (or someone else's, if that's where I'm directing it to) and my awareness and inner senses open as if I am in the body. Information comes to me about the body and can I sense how it is healing and changing.

Exercise I

Sit or lay in a quiet space and connect to your upper chest (sacred or spiritual heart), intend to send energy (healing frequency) to your nervous system. You may feel a sensation of flow from your heart and a calming, healing feeling. You may sense how much your nervous system needs this healing and other possible information about that system. When you feel complete, You can stop transmitting the energy (which continues to run for a while on it's own) and you will likely feel a change, relief, balance and knowing a healing occurred. It will always create positive change and healing for your highest good. It will never do "nothing" regardless of what you experience. The more you practice, the easier you will get impressions and information from your body through inner seeing, feeling, hearing and knowing. You will know what is going on in your body, why (the root cause) and run the frequency to begin the self healing.

Exercise II

If you feel a virus coming on, you can send this heart frequency to your blood, as it runs, the connection gets stronger and your inner senses of seeing, feeling, hearing knowing are present. You can sense or feel as you internally scan your blood to see if there is a virus or bacteria present.

I felt feverish and not well and knew there was a virus. I ran the heart frequency to scan my blood and was aware of a flu virus. I was also aware of the frequency cleaning my blood. It does require a deep inner focus and concentration to be aware of what is occurring internally. It's similar to meditation. As you run heart frequency, it puts you into a meditative state and automatically begins the healing. It took about 1 hour to fully clear the virus, as I tuned in again, I sensed the virus and bacteria were gone. How did I know this? The same inner awareness (senses) showed me in a feeling, sensing, seeing (inner vision) and knowing it was gone.

I felt a huge relief, fever was gone and felt fine afterwards and never got a flu or cold.

I run heart frequency regularly to my entire body and check the blood often to sense if it is clean. You can also clear out environmental toxins, free radicals, yeast, etc. with heart frequency.

This highly intelligent frequency knows what to do as you send it and doesn't need your belief or you "doing" it. As a reiki master, I find quantum energy (heart frequency) very different than reiki. Reiki is amazing and I love it. It feels very different to me than quantum energy. I love them both and use them together, but I find I can work with very specific issues and get an inner connection and communication that I don't with reiki. They work very well together and by using reiki first my connect to the quantum energy is easier.

After working with many clients and myself, I learned to send the quantum heart frequency to "root cause, priority" which will go to the root of the problem. Sometimes the problem or pain is in one area but the cause of the problem originates somewhere else. The energy takes me to where it starts and I watch as the energy moves from one place to another in the body as it heals it in priority sequence. It has its own intelligence and knows how to work with the energy of the body for the highest good.

The problem or issue that I am able to sense or see in the body is what is being balanced or healed. I don't need to know what the problem is to heal it. Running the energy will show me what the problem is and the core of it.

Out of all the modalities I am trained in, quantum energy healing has changed my life the most and that of my students and clients.

Life Story

When I put my back out, I was in so much pain I could hardly move. I remembered (the pain distracted me and I forgot for a while) that I can use the quantum heart frequency and began sending it to the area where the pain was. I felt energy movement in the area where the pain was and a shift in my back occured that I could feel. The pain was gone as the bone was moved back into place. Quantum energy supports your energy field in moving itself into alignment.

You can scan yourself regularly and practice using this energy and see what you experience.

Running the frequency of the heart will help you to connect within; to the consciousness of your body. Your body is very intelligent, knows how to heal itself and you can talk to any body part and listen to what it's saying to you. Does it hold an emotion or does it need a diet change? Ask and it will tell you. Please don't judge your body, it affects your energy field.

The lower frequency of pain and imbalance is positively influenced by the high frequency of quantum energy heart frequency.

SHIFTING FREQUENCIES

How to Raise your frequency

A method I learned on how to raise my frequency is to work with breath. I imagine opening my body top to bottom like a pipe. I connect to the Earth below and ground by imagining a cord or string from my sacral chakra to Earth and my root chakra to Earth . Then I begin breathing energy from Earth up my feet and into my body and out the top of my head. I repeat this until I feel very grounded, balanced and present. Next, I connect to the higher realms and source/God etc. above by sending a stream of energy from my crown until I feel connected to source. I expand my energy field (aura) as wide as feels right for me, even wider than the Earth. Expansion brings connection and relaxation, fear creates contraction.

Then I begin breathing light from far above my head as I intend to connect to source, breathe it into my body and anchor it into my hands/feet and cells of my body. I continue to breathe in light from above and anchor it into myself until I feel joy, peace, expansion and connection to my Higher Self. I also breathe in the energy of my higher self with intention as I am breathing.

The higher self part of you is all knowing about you, your life and has all the answers to any questions you may have. It is you, but the highest most expanded and connected version of you. When you are in this connected, expanded state you are able to see and know from the perspective of your higher self rather than from your human self.

CHAPTER 2

TRANSFORMATION TECHNIQUES

When we are going through a transition from the old identity to the new, we can experience anxiety, stress, frustration and feeling disconnected from the world. As this was happening to me I needed tools to work with to help me stay balanced.

A favourite technique is **7 second breathing**. If you are needing to release anxiety breathe in to the count of 7 seconds, hold for 1 count and breathe out to the count of 7 seconds. Repeat until you feel relaxed and centered. This has truly helped me during my transformation of releasing my old reality.

A second technique that I love that works well for anxiety release is **Heart breathing or Heavenly breathing**. During meditation time put you focus on your sacred or spiritual heart in the upper chest. You relax deeply and focus on the heart and away from the mind. You intend to allow the heart to "breathe". You let go of the breathing process and continue to focus on the sacred heart. As this happens your breathing may change, stop for a while or alter in some way. Once I let go and my sacred heart was "breathing" me I moved into a blissful state out of the mind and connected to my higher self. I was no longer thinking or responding as my ego self but was heart centred, peaceful and in thoughtless awareness.

I continue to practice and obtain varying degrees of the bliss and clear mind and it's the most calming method I know of.

SHIFTING FREQUENCIES

Message from Archangel Raphael

Greetings, it is I Archangel Raphael at your service. It is indeed a time of "letting go" above all else. YOU are being prepared for what is to come. We, the Archangels, Masters and those of the light are working with you continuously adjusting your energy fields to hold more light.

You are being encouraged to release all that no longer serves you and accept the fact that you are truly magnificent beings who are capable of creating the world you want. Just let go of what is "heavy" to you and watch your world transform before your eyes. All that you let go of will be replaced by something "more" than you may have imagined. It is indeed difficult times for many of you and we see the suffering and struggle. However, it is in your hands how long you wish the struggle to continue. You can open your hands to us and ask us to take the "heaviness" in your life and transform it. We will oblige happily.

As your load gets lighter energetically, the signs, synchronicities and opportunities you are wanting will begin to appear. Just call upon me, Archangel Raphael or any of the other Archangels or Masters (of love and light) and there is much we can do to assist you. Remember to ask, we will never interfere without your request.

Quantum Healing Stories

My Mom's pet bird was sick; she said "he doesn't look good at all, I would really miss him if he passed away." Can you run the quantum energy for him? So I did and as I ran it, I could sense that he had a fever and bacteria in his stomach related to what he was eating. He loves cheese and eats too much of it. After the session he was much better and recovered that same day. My Mom was so happy and so was I.

I find that animals heals very fast, quicker than humans, when working with quantum heart frequency.

I was working with a friend's cat who wasn't eating. She didn't know why so as I ran the energy, I sensed a blockage in her esophagus. The energy cleared it out and the cat was fine within a short time and eating again. This saved a vet bill and potential stress and suffering for the cat.

When working with quantum energy, it is able to go inside, find the root cause of the problem and begins to supports the body to heal itself. It begins to change the energy field of the body bringing it back into balance and health.

I was doing a session for a client and as I ran the energy I could see there was a twist in her spine, which it balanced. It aligned the body head to toe and she is able to walk easier and no longer has the pain that was once there.

I am creating a community of healers connecting worldwide, sharing healing, learning and working with quantum energy.

I asked my Guides and Angels years ago what my purpose was, and they said that one of the reasons I am here is to bring through the higher frequencies and make them accessible to others. I feel like I'm fulfilling my mission by connecting others to quantum heart frequency and showing them what is possible. My soul's purpose is to help people release physical and emotional pain and heal themselves so they can be free to live their life purpose. The fastest way I know of to accomplish this is using the frequency of the heart.

◆ PART II ◆

SHIFTING FREQUENCIES THROUGH FOOD

Most people have some form of addiction and for many it's food or sugar.

This is a major trap that keeps you stuck, imbalanced and not able to move forward.

Do you feel tired & sick all the time? Have brain fog, bloating, and crave sugar?

No matter what you do, you can't get past it?

I was there. I had "chronic fatigue syndrome" which really was candida or yeast overgrowth, for many years.

Most books on Candida focus on diet and the physical aspect of this imbalance. However the balancing of the body is first and foremost an "inside job."

This means the imbalance or illness is due to a combination of what you feel, believe, your lifestyle, your relationship with others and yourself and unhealed trauma.

Candida (and any other disease] is simply the body's expression of what is going on internally with you. By its nature, yeast is parasitic and demands to be fed.

You will create an imbalance or illness to show you what you need to learn about yourself.

By giving your power away to others, giving too much of your energy, putting yourself last; you become drained. By continually giving away your energy and not receiving enough back, your system will go on overload and imbalances such as chronic Fatigue, candida and fibromyalgia occur.

Having had yeast overgrowth and sugar addiction over a period of many years, I finally found all the pieces to the puzzle. I learned how to heal my body naturally and get my energy and life back! I will show you how so you can too.

Note: using the information in this book can help you heal other illnesses besides candida.

Candida is an imbalance of yeast, fed by too much sugar in the system. If left unchecked the results can be: Fatigue, flu like symptoms, brain fog, depression, systemic candida, leaky gut syndrome, weakened immune, food allergies, indigestion etc.

Most people don't know it's all from Candida; they're being controlled and it's running their life!

I didn't know what was wrong, I had no energy, no life and was depressed all the time. I tried everything to get better and I did to a certain point, **but it always came back, WHY?**

After 17 years of studying and trying everything I finally found all the pieces to the puzzle!

Part of the missing link is healing inner trauma, forgiveness and taking your power back, so the body heals itself. The outer manifestation of illness is always connected to inner unresolved issues. No matter what you do, the illness returns until you do the inner work.

I learned how to eliminate candida permanently and how to find the emotional root cause of it and how to clear it.

I healed myself after having chronic fatigue and candida for more than 15 years!

NO MORE SUGAR CRAVINGS!

"I feel totally different. I'm in control of my eating, I don't crave sugar at night anymore, I'm free!" -Annett S.

MY HEALING JOURNEY

My healing journey was my wake up call to life. I was disconnected from myself, my health and my true calling. It took the label chronic fatigue syndrome to get my attention. It was impressive sounding and the perfect vehicle for me to play the "victim" role. It seemed so much easier not taking responsibility for my life and using the label as an excuse to play small. For me it was necessary to hit rock bottom before I would wake up to the truth; I am the creator of my life and my body has its own inner physician much more powerful than any Doctor.

After seven years of feeling unwell I found the source of the problem; which was diet and digestion related. This was when I first heard about candida and what it can do to your system once it becomes systemic (in the blood).

Through self-study I learned how to correct this yeast overgrowth. The challenge was dealing with addiction to sugar. One of the hardest things I have ever done was to get off sugar to become free of the vicious cycle of an acidic system and feeding yeast with sugar. It took hard work to clear my body of sugar addiction and yeast overgrowth.

Within a few months of removing sugar, wheat, yeast (especially bread) I felt like a new person! I finally found out what was wrong and how to fix it!

Note: doing a candida cleanse and changing diet is crucial and then creating an internal environment where yeast overgrowth cannot live. (By taking acidophilus and enzymes, I recommend Future Formulations Enzymes, your body will then be able to keep the yeast in check on its own). I found that Colloidal Silver (Essential Silver brand) really works to clear excess yeast from the body!

Note: The excess yeast will clear if you are eating a proper diet and avoiding sugar while taking colloidal silver! After cleansing and when you are balanced you can eat some fruit, honey, molasses etc. and natural sugars. (In moderation; focus on keeping sugar levels balanced at all times).

I would plan to avoid white/brown sugar for life, once you have had candida it will quickly come back if you eat sugar again. (Even natural sugars if in excess).

It is vital to learn to balance the sugar levels through proper diet. However, the most important thing is understanding why candida showed up in your reality in the first place. Candida and parasites "demand to be fed". The imbalance always originates from inside (what is going on with you) first.

Where are you giving away your power and allowing others to take from you?

Do you have a death wish on some level?

These are some questions to ask yourself; take the journey and begin searching within for the answers.

As you begin to see a pattern forming begin by making necessary changes to how you perceive yourself and others and what identity you believe yourself to have.

Choosing a new identity is key. Releasing the old identity and label of being sick, just by doing this alone helps the healing begin.

Choice is powerful and also what you believe.

◆ CHAPTER 3 ◆

BOUNDARIES

Set up healthy boundaries where your needs are met, you are not giving away your energy, and you are receiving and giving in a balanced way. The energy vibration of the problem or illness (parasites) has a matching vibration to your own in some way, which is why it appeared to you rather than some other illness. Close the door to parasitic energy, you don't need approval from outside yourself.

Stop searching outside of yourself to get energy or fulfillment; accept yourself as good enough. The love you seek is inside yourself, nothing is missing. No one can drain you or take your energy if you don't "need" anything from them. Healthy relationships are nourishing but "neediness" puts us in a place of disempowerment.

With self-love and self-acceptance, view yourself as just as important, powerful, valuable and acceptable as anyone else. Learn how to monitor your energy and not "give until it hurts". Listen to your body so as not to burn out the adrenals.

Supplements, sleep, adrenal support and bringing the body back into balance is needed. Once the cravings for sugar are gone, you are in control again and on your way to wellness. Working on the subconscious level to change negative beliefs is immensely helpful in changing your perspective.

I believe we create everything we experience in our life because of how we think and what we believe. So I began to deal with the emotional cause. I needed to release the identity and drop the label of this dis-ease. I later discovered that parts of me wanted to keep it! (not wanting to take responsibility for my life as a whole and powerful being). **Fear of having to step forward in my life.**

As I was searching for ways to heal myself I discovered reiki and hypnotherapy.

Part of the solution was to clear all emotional connections to the problem (needing the problem in some way) for the healing to be complete. I became a hypnotherapist/Reiki Master and learned how to use the power of the subconscious mind. By working with these healing tools my true transformation began. Once the lesson is learned from the issue/illness that showed up, it is free to go.

I realized I hated the "yeast" parasites for taking so much from me and had to forgive it as if it were a person. This 'dark night of the soul' experience was needed in order for me to wake up to my true purpose. I was forced to go on a journey within and face myself.

Close the door to parasitic people, situations and energies. Release struggle, self sabotage, self punishment and self denial.

Trust yourself and be your true authentic self.

Release patterns of limiting the self for fear of failure and playing it safe. Being ill is a handy distraction to not having to be responsible in your life and stepping forward into empowerment.

It can feel much safer to stay sick!

Aha! Once you are aware of this you can begin to dismantle the illness and the body heals itself. Begin to release: **"Being sick is safe"**

A process I used to do this was:

- Ask yourself: what lessons did I learn and what gifts did I receive from this illness/problem? (Personally, I learned to set boundaries and not let others take from me. Taking my power back, trusting myself and feeling good enough and "worthy").

- Forgive the illness/person/thing, whatever it is completely – knowing that you created the situation to learn the lessons and receive the gifts. (I had to actually forgive the yeast as if it were a person and release all anger, as anger would not allow it to heal).

- I spoke to the yeast saying "Thank-you for the gifts and lessons you gave me. I no longer need you; I release you, forgive you and set you free. You are free to go your way and I am free to go mine. Check on a scale of 1 to 10 if you have really forgiven all of it. Also, I forgive myself (for creating the situation) and set myself free. Release the identity of it. **Did you learn the lesson? Releasing "being sick is safe?"**

- Connect with and send healing to the sacral chakra (belly area: related to sexuality, creativity, expression) and root chakra (related to feeling supported, money, career, empowerment). I finally felt emotionally, spiritually, mentally and physically free of candida.

Note: One of the most important things I learned was to see the yeast overgrowth as an "umbrella" of protection to show you when you are out of balance in your life and to nurture yourself!

SELF-IDENTITY

Your outer reality reflects your inner beliefs and self image you have. Hold the image and **"transformational vibration" (feeling/energy with focused intention)** *on how you wish your body to be. Do not be concerned with symptoms or how you situation/health appears now, but simply keep affirming the image and state of being you prefer (regardless of how you feel at the moment!). By doing so, you literally shift "realities" and your body begins to reflect your inner state of being. Your body WILL follow suit by transforming into the state of being (health) if you hold this intention internally at all times.*

You can use this statement out loud during the day as a reminder: **"Circumstances don't matter, only state of being matters, what state of being do I prefer? (And then behave that way!).**

(Reference: Daryl Anka/Bashar: Youtube). Behave as if the body is in complete balance and health. Do not judge your health based on your current circumstances or experience, simply allow it to transform by holding your "state of being" as you wish it to be. This will take some practice, the biggest challenge being not to react when you experience symptoms of the old imbalance. However, if you affirm the statement to yourself out loud and continue to hold the intention, the body will simply heal itself. The mind and judging yourself keeps the imbalance. Keep your focus on your image/vision/feeling/intention on complete health. Do not "peek" at your health (symptoms) and affirm: "see it's not working, it's still there...

Hold the intent and affirmation regardless. The body will reflect back what you are affirming internally. You are creating your reality. The more responsible and aware you become internally, the more your life, health and energy will flow. **Release all judgment of your situation (health/problems etc.) this only makes it stick. Make peace with it, become neutral and continue to focus on the way you desire it to be (BE THAT).**

Important note: Release the "poor me" identity, suffering and being unwell to "being safe". Follow a candida diet if you crave sugar or have severe symptoms: bloating, fever, fatigue, brain fog etc. When the sugar cravings are gone, your yeast levels are back in balance. Once you learn to love and accept yourself, listen to your body, and not give your energy away your body will stay balanced automatically.

HOW VS. WHAT YOU EAT

What is your relationship with yourself? What is your relationship with food and nurturing yourself? Do you take time to honour your body, prepare the food that your body wants, bless it and then really enjoy it?

Your body has its own intelligence; you can speak to it and it will communicate with you. Ask it what it needs and then sit quietly and listen, the answer can come in many forms. A feeling, a thought, an image. Pay Attention to what your body is telling you and begin to form a positive relationship with it.

Do you eat only when you are hungry and stop when you are full?

Do you multitask or eat when you're in a hurry? A large percentage of how well you are able to digest will be based upon what you are thinking, feeling and doing at the time of eating. Release all judgements of yourself, the food and your body! Make friends with the food on your plate; love it and bless it, this prepares it for you to receive.

So many people are in a love-hate relationship with food. Food is then used to numb unwanted emotions rather than feeling them. Each time this happens the body stores that emotion causing blockages in the system emotionally and energetically.

Are you feeling anxious, stressed, angry or any other negative emotion? Rather than reach for food, Stop, become very aware, feel that feeling without the need to do anything about it. Then ask yourself, what do I need at this moment? Maybe it's a walk, or to phone a friend or some other loving kindness to yourself. When you are in touch with yourself and your body, you will take in the right kinds and amounts of food best for you. You will automatically remain slim, digest your food well and be healthier.

If you are in a struggle with your body and food and eat based on emotion, not true hunger, you disconnect yourself from that communication with your body. The hungry and full signals will be indistinguishable. Toxins and emotions are stored in the fat cells, why not drain them of the stored emotion and the fat can begin to melt away? Rather than emotional-based eating, feel that emotion (don't numb it) and take your power back! Each time you do this, you strengthen the positive relationship and communication between you and your body.

Step one: ask your body what it needs and listen.
Step two: eat only when you are truly hungry.
Step three: make friends with your food, bless and love it.
Step four: eat slowly and be fully present, don't multitask.

Step five: put your awareness on your belly and be conscious of the digestion

Process.

More than anything else, this process will serve you to be healthy, slim and have a positive relationship with food and yourself.

◆ CHAPTER 4 ◆

RECHARGING YOUR SYSTEMS, ORGANS AND CHAKRAS

Did you know you can talk to your body; it is a living, intelligent organism and it will respond. It hears everything you're thinking and feeling and creates health or disease, based on what is happening inside you.

You can recharge all of your systems, organs and energy centres known as chakras. Simply imagine plugging in all of your systems: immune system, central nervous system,etc. into a supercharger in the wall. Imagination and intention is a powerful way to heal and communicate with the body.

Just like you would plug in an electrical appliance. Imagine each system being plugged in one by one and begin to talk to your body. Imagine and intend that each system is being super charged and healed, functioning perfectly.

Feel the positive energy going into each system recharging and balancing them. Have an inner conversation with your body, talk to it and tell it: you are now being supercharged for a super healthy immune, digestive, nervous system etc.

Begin imagining bringing healing energy in from the earth, oxygenating the body and flooding it with positive emotions. Begin to breathe joy, harmony, peace, wellness, and balance into every cell of your body.

Breathe in deeply into the belly, feeling the flood of positive emotions as your systems are being recharged! Breathe in joy (or any other positive emotion you choose) and feel and visualize the body lighting up from the inside with healing life force.

Next begin to talk to your organs. Asking each one if there's anything that it needs. For example your liver may need to release some anger. Imagine the liver opening, releasing and draining any stored anger, grief trauma etc. Ask your organs what colour it would like to be bathed in. For example, the Lungs may like to be bathed in a happy, sunny yellow colour.

Try on each colour in your imagination on the organ and see what feels best to you; that is the colour to use. Then just imagine the Organ absorbing the healing properties of that colour. Ask the organ if it is happy or sad or if there's something you can do for it. Each organ is alive, has its own consciousness and stores memory in its cells.

If there was a trauma one of your organs or body parts may have stored that memory. By getting to know your body and speaking to it daily, much healing can occur.

Flood your body from head to toe with life force energy allowing it to clear any blocked energy. This will go a long way to keeping you healthy.

Imagine each of the 7 main Chakras receiving light, Clearing and supercharging them. Just as a vehicle requires maintenance, so does your physical vessel.

YOU CREATED IT, YOU CAN UNCREATE IT!

When you are ready to take full responsibility for yourself, you will be able to turn things around. If you continue to blame others for your situation, you are continually giving your power away. Everything that you are experiencing was created by you, for your highest good, to learn and grow.

The sooner you're able to see the truth of this, the quicker you will be able to harness your body's ability to heal itself.

SHIFTING FREQUENCIES

It is easy to get wrapped up in the story of who we feel we are. It feels very justified to complain and talk about it and identify with it. And maybe it is justified, but it works to your detriment. Remember to forgive someone no matter what they did, more for yourself so you can heal and move forward. You don't want to stay tied to that person or event. Even though you may be right, forgive anyway for your health.

***Check in with yourself to see where you feel that you are getting something out of the imbalance the illness the suffering etc. (holding onto it because you believe it helps you in some way).**

Be honest with yourself and you will see a pattern. does it feel safe to be unwell, not having to take responsibility for yourself? Does it feel comfortable and familiar? Is there a fear of moving forward and becoming everything that you know you can be?

If you truly want to be healthy and well, it starts with being honest with yourself. Once you're able to identify these patterns, you can look them squarely in the eye and then let them go!

This will begin a very powerful process of self healing and creating a new self identity. How you see yourself and what you believe yourself to be is the key. Change this inside of yourself and your outer reality, including your body and health will change as well.

As much as you may wish to believe otherwise, all experiences were created by you, based on what you believe about yourself and traumas/unforgiveness. If you feel there is a benefit or deserve to suffer and be unhealthy, this is what you will experience.

To create the changes you're looking for, begin by being honest with yourself and take a very good look at yourself. Why did you create this illness or imbalance? What needs to be learned here about yourself?

Begin a daily, quiet inner, contemplation and meditation practice. Even just a few minutes a day of going within and connecting to yourself, will serve you well to create what you want.

You hold the key to unlock the door, to free yourself and re-create your life.

You created your experience; when you are ready, you can un-create your situation and build a new one. It takes being aware, courage and being willing to step out of the comfort zone. All very doable, if that is your choice.

MEDITATION AND SELF-HYPNOSIS

There is no better place to look than inside of yourself, for the answers to the questions that you're looking for. You are the authority on you and you need to trust yourself to get your guidance from within.

When you want to create change in your life, the first place to look is inside yourself. Take time every day to sit and practice clearing the thoughts and just observe the mind and it's chattering state without needing to do anything about it.

As you observe, the space between the thoughts will become longer and you will experience more peace and quiet in your mind.

When I want an answer to a question in my life, I sit quietly and begin to sing the word HU as a toning mantra. As in one long word as in: Huuuuu....This clears my mind and connects me to my soul.

After about 15 to 20 minutes of toning with this word, I sit quietly in contemplation. I ask a question about my life and sit quietly and receive a feeling, thought, image, word etc. Often I will receive an answer to my question right away, but sometimes it comes later.

When you ask for help from your inner guidance, soul, guides, angels etc. and relax and let go, the help is sure to come. Be open to watching for synchronicity, information and help from any source that is coming to you. When you relax and get out of your own way, you receive assistance.

When we try to force things in our life or stress over the answer to a problem, this blocks the energy flow. You will see that by asking for assistance, letting go, and then expecting the answer to come, it will every time.

SHIFTING FREQUENCIES

Ask for help with releasing cravings, ask for help with clearing negative beliefs, negative patterns, negative thoughts, negative self talk and negative people from your life etc. The way will be shown to you, if you stay open in positive expectancy.

Another very powerful tool would be that of self hypnosis. Simply by relaxing the body and slowing down the mind. for example counting backwards from 100 to 1 will put you in the alpha or theta state. Once in this state you can access the subconscious mind where the negative beliefs, fears, and negative patterns are.

With daily practice, you can get good at this and examine the negative blocks/beliefs as they arise. You can access the subconscious mind to release these negative patterns or beliefs and choose other more self-supporting ones in their place.

In this quiet place in the mind you can also ask, what is the true source of this problem? It will pop in your mind very quickly and subtly, it's important not to discount what comes to you.

Because we live in such a busy, fast-moving world, we need to take time daily to clear the mind and unload all that has been downloaded into us. For example, stimuli from TV, other people, jobs, and just general over-stimulation in a fast-paced world. With over-thinking and mind chaos we are no longer in control. With a clear mind, we can we start to become in control of our lives again and create the reality that we want.

With inner clarity by practising daily meditation or self-hypnosis, you will find the answers to your questions and can start to create the changes you want.

When changing from the inside out from the root source of the issue, the changes will be permanent.

◆ CHAPTER 5 ◆

NURTURE AND NOURISH

Close the door to the program that you created to learn from. Give yourself permission to be nourished by the foods that you eat and also the lifestyle that you live. Release any and all patterns of self punishment self judgement or the belief that; I can't heal my body because someone has wronged me or it's unsafe to be well (it forces you out of your comfort zone!)

Release any beliefs of I'm a bad girl or a bad boy and don't deserve the best. This is based on past experiences and wounds, not on the truth of what and who you truly are.

Your outer reality reflects your inner beliefs and self image you have of yourself.

Continue to hold the feeling and focus (frequency) what you prefer in your health and body. Then act and feel that way now. Keep holding the focus, feelings and vibration or (frequency) of what you want your health to be like, regardless of outside appearance for example, symptoms that may appear.

Your body will follow suit by transforming into the frequency, state of being and health that you desire if you keep affirming the feeling, focus and frequency and allow yourself to be transformed.

Do not judge your health based on your current circumstances, symptoms or experience; simply allow it to transform by holding your state of being, (energetic vibration) feelings and image on complete health.

Remember, do not peek and affirm "see it's not working it's still there"...

Hold the intent and feelings regardless of what is happening on the outside. The body will heal itself as it only reflects back what you hold inside. You create your reality.

Release all judgement of yourself and health issue, problem etc. this only makes it stick. Make peace with your body and health issue, become neutral and continue to focus on the way you desire it to be, and be that!

FORGIVENESS

Self-healing is an inside job: it's all about you and taking your power back. Regardless of what someone else has done, or what someone else believes, or what someone else's issues are. You're not responsible to help others change or heal, but you are responsible for your own transformation and healing.

Release the past; give yourself permission to be healthy and to feel safe to move forward. Release all patterns of feeling rejected and therefore rejecting the self. Release victim hood, move into empowerment accepting yourself. Honour yourself and your feelings. You cannot play the role of victim and be empowered and successfully living your life purpose at the same time.

If someone hurt you, no matter what they did, forgive and release them. This does not mean they did not hurt you; forgiveness is a gift to yourself so that you can heal and move forward.

By not forgiving, you stay connected to that person or situation that hurt you, thereby holding you back. Who was right or wrong does not matter, what matters is that by forgiving you are able to heal and move on.

Do you really want to stay connected to that person or situation and stay stuck? This is what not forgiving does.

You may be fully justified in your anger and not forgiving, but it does not serve you. Do whatever it takes to forgive and let it go, no matter how difficult. Only then will you truly be free and healthy. Do it in steps if you need to, but DO IT! (If you want complete health).

Note: If you're willing to do this, no matter how difficult, you will be giving yourself the biggest gift of all and will be able to move forward into health and live your purpose.

SUPPLEMENTS AND DIET

Colloidal silver 1 teaspoon or tablespoon (if you want it stronger, listen to your body) 2 X per day. (You may have yeast die off symptoms & feel worse for a while as your body is balancing). The liquid silver kills excess yeast, bacteria and lots more. Very gentle on the body. It does not kill the good bacteria like oregano oil does.

**VERY IMPORTANT: TAKE THE SILVER LONG TERM IF NEEDED UNTIL YOU ARE BALANCED. When symptoms are gone, you can go off the silver. Repeat again if needed.

- Enzymes **FUTURE FORMULATION Brand (EATS EXCESS YEAST!!)**
- **Betain Hydrochloride HCL (digestion/bloating) if needed
- Probiotic per meal
- aloe Vera for elimination (helps with constipation)
- magnesium oxide powder (assists with elimination) I buy Now Brand.
- easy Iron (Platinum Brand, does not constipate) for anemia (if you have low iron)
- Vitamin C for immune & elimination, Liquid Vitamin B (for Energy)
- Concentrace liquid minerals assists with (elimination)
- chromium tablets (to balance blood sugar levels)

Vaginal yeast infection: tablespoon apple cider vinegar (I like Bragg's) mixed with water, diluted enough so it's not too strong, use as a douche. Repeat often as necessary to clear it up. You can also take a 1/4 teaspoon of baking soda in water (ingested orally). You can use tea tree oil in the vagina if there is severe pain, but not daily. (use sparingly) as it throws off the vaginal chemistry balance if used too often.

PLEASE HYDRATE: Dehydration causes extreme fatigue/brain fog, drink enough water!! Personally, I like Kangen water, try to get a good water system.

Dr. Schulze bowel cleanse is very effective in cleansing the bowel, I highly recommend it. Ordered online. 1-800-HERB-DOC for more information on cleanses. (These cleanses save lives)

You need to have bowel movements two to three times per day, GET DOWN IN A SQUAT TO REACTIVATE YOUR BODY'S BOWEL MOVEMENTS (UNTIL YOU HAVE A MOVEMENT). Increase Magnesium Oxide powder until you have easy bowel movements. Anywhere from 1 teaspoon per day or more.

Increase future formulation enzymes if triggered with severe symptoms such as brain fog etc. and sugar cravings!

Please follow the Candida diet. Look it up on line or get a book etc. The following is a short overview of the main points:

Avoid bread, wheat, yeast, sugar, dairy, mushrooms, honey, syrup, dried fruit, fruit, flour, potatoes, corn, popcorn, chips, junk food, pastries and flours.

If you crave sugar, don't have any forms of sugar until you balance your blood sugar levels with proper diet and supplementation. You may eat brown rice, Millan, Quinoa, Whole grains, eggs, meat, nuts, seeds, vegetables, fish, coconut butter, olive oil etc.

If Emotions come up when clearing candida, allow them to be there, feel them fully without doing anything about it. This neutralizes the emotions and releases the pattern.

Don't stuff or avoid the negative emotion that only keeps it stuck in you and the health issue remains.

Releasing negative trapped emotions and forgiveness allows the body to heal and Yeast levels automatically balance. It's natural to have some yeast in the system, just not in excess where imbalance then occurs.

Remember: candida (or any other chronic illness or disease) is a messenger to teach you where you are not in balance, not taking care of yourself and giving your power away!

It's time to make the changes and take your power back. You can do it.

If you need assistance in moving forward, group quantum healing transformation, private sessions/coaching for physical and emotional healing & pain relief are available.

◆ PART III ◆

SHIFTING FREQUENCIES WITH THOUGHT

The information presented was telepathically transmitted to the author from Master Kuthumi. The topic was chosen by Kuthumi and is sometimes written in unconventional language. This is the style in which the information was brought through and every effort was made to keep the original material as unaltered as possible.

It is often written in third person (we) meaning the collective consciousness of the Ascended Masters and all those who serve the light (or God).

By reading this information you will connect with Kuthumi and a shift to a higher consciousness will be possible. If you choose this path, Kuthumi can assist you on your journey.

"What the mind holds, it creates. If the mind holds positivity it will create the same reality for the thinker. By design, you were created to be the authority in your life and have the answers and solutions to every situation that could possibly arise, simply by listening to the small inner voice. Peace of mind leads to literally creating a better reality for us all; one that is free of destruction, chaos, negativity and fear. Learn how to clean up our thought pollution and create a new Earth. Peace on Earth first begins with peace of mind." -Kuthumi

THERE IS A WORLD INSIDE
****

There is a world inside that will show you the way
There is a world inside that will show you who you are
There is a world inside that will bring you peace
There is a world inside that loves you as you are
There is a world inside that will bring you more
When you tap this world inside, you will feel the change
This world inside is part of who you are
Be ready for this world inside; it's time to visit there
You see this world inside will change your very soul
This world inside is your very own.
In this world feel yourself be free
In this world inside is infinite possibility
This world inside is part of who you are let this world
Inside shine brighter than a star!
When you visit this world inside take me with you there
In this world inside all can join us there
In this world inside you will smile without a care
Everyday your world inside expands why not
Visit there and see what you will find?
It's all inside of you; why not see what you will find?

****

-Annett Schneider

LIVE YOUR SOUL'S PURPOSE

When a person is ready for change the tool appears. This information is such a tool. Prepare yourself for the changes that will take place as you read this and practice the exercises. Taming the mind is a challenge but a most worthy goal. As you gain control of your mind you gain control of your life.

As the Earth and people are moving through their grand shift to a higher consciousness and state of being, it is time to go within and seek out your own wisdom. I encourage you to take the time daily to quiet the mind and listen to your inner guidance.

SHIFTING FREQUENCIES

As my spirit guides say: it is easy to get distracted by the outside world and get pulled away from meditation time in a flash! As you take the time to go within your life will run more smoothly, you will see the synchronicities and become inspired to live your soul's purpose.

Begin daily to call on your Angels/guides and Higher Self to work with you in meditation. Request that you be cleared of old programming and receive assistance to move through your blocks. When you begin to quiet your mind you will experience resistance from your ego self. The part that does not like change and wants to be in control at all times.

As my Angel "Perelondra" says you will reach the "boiling point" where anxiety and fear crop up during meditation. As you persist you will move beyond it and into the "void" a place of complete bliss and infinite possibility.

Allow yourself to observe the anxiety without doing anything about it. Focus on the space between the thoughts and bring yourself back to the present moment. With daily meditation you will connect with your Higher Self and will begin to find your way home to yourself. Following this inner guidance will help you live your true soul's purpose. Have the courage to look inside; you will be glad you did.

THE DESIRED OUTCOME FULFILLS ITSELF

"All things are meant to be easy; it's people who make it difficult! Enjoy each day as it comes without there having to be a definite outcome for the day. Let it be okay as it is and enjoy the process. As you do this the desired outcome fulfills itself!

-Annett's Guides

HOW THIS INFORMATION CAN HELP YOU

Learning to meditate and control your thoughts is the most important skill you can learn. How and what you think inside is a direct reflection of what you are manifesting on the outside (your reality).

This information can help you turn your life around, if you choose to. If you are stuck in a groove (old pattern) and feel like you can't get out;

go to the source of the problem. Look inside yourself first, and then I assure you, you will see the light at the end of the tunnel.

Letting go of the grip you have on life, and taking a step back to do some inventory of how you think, will be the biggest bonus you could ever receive. Do you want to create something different? It starts with your thoughts. By using the methods outlined here, you have a map to begin to see the changes that you so desire in your life.

By taking complete responsibility and learning to quiet the mind through meditation and clearing techniques, you will see a new person forming before your eyes!

If you have truly had enough of your old life and would like to begin anew, start to work with your thoughts, and allow it to work for you. When you are in a mode of self-empowerment you can achieve whatever you want. Your mind is the key.

You may think you need someone or something else in order to make it. However, every tool you need is inside of you. At this you can feel relief because you don't need anything from anyone in order to break free. You simply need to decide what you want and love yourself enough to make the changes (starting from the inside). Discipline is required. By releasing anxiety, fear, and self-sabotage I was able to create the life I want.

You can choose to begin again by using the tools in this book assisting you to move forward. Connecting with others who are where you want to be will help you on your journey.

For true healing to happen, going within (meditation), connecting with your purpose and being aware of what is going on in your thoughts and beliefs are required. Learning how to tame the mind and use it as the powerful tool it was meant to be, rather than allowing it to be in control of you is what you will learn.

◆ CHAPTER 6 ◆

TAMING THE MIND

I am the Master Kuthumi at your service. It is my great delight to be invited to write this book. My hope is that with this knowledge there will come an understanding of what the mind is to be used for. As most of you are unaware, the mind is being misused. By this I mean that it is being overused and underused at the same time. It is being overused in that it is being "held hostage" by your continual stream of thoughts. This creates a blockage in the way that it could be used. My advice to you all is to SLOW DOWN your thoughts and your activities! When the mind is over-used it tends to shut down in the sense that it can no longer function at optimal performance.

Imagine now, if you will, someone whose thoughts and emotions are at their control and not the other way around. This person has learned to control what comes in and out of their mind. For most of us this is not the case; we are under the control of the mind and its constant chattering! The task of taming the mind is a simple yet challenging one. Once fully harnessed there is not a more powerful tool to be found.

Step number one is to be aware of what is going on in the mind at all times. Once you are aware you are able to edit what stays and what goes. This is of utmost importance in the sense that what the mind holds, it creates. If the mind holds positivity it will create the same reality for the thinker. The time is coming, dear ones, when mastership over the mind will be of immense value.

Understand dear ones that your mind holds the key to all that you desire. Stop looking outside of yourselves for the answers; truly it is from inside that the real power lies. Let me paint you a picture: At one time in your history all was well with the people and their ability to have a fully functioning mind. Then one day it began to go downhill and negativity was introduced into the stream of consciousness. And of course negativity has a way of spreading itself around. This of course creates all kinds of other problems that manifest themselves into your realities. And thus the pattern was set for the mind to create disease, burden, lack and the list is endless. So here we find ourselves in the present day with a mess to clean up. The mind has literally created pollutants on every level and every form. Time to clean up the mess, dear ones.

And so I am offered this opportunity to speak to you in this way that you will understand and learn. I offer you my sympathy; difficult is the journey for those who have not mastered their thoughts. However it is fully under your control. All that is required is a little thought-watching and a lot of releasing the negative from your repertoire of thoughts. Never under-estimate the power of the thinking process. When energy is allowed to flow in a free-flowing way, thinking becomes clear and effortless with knowledge and wisdom coming to you at just the right time. However, currently most of you overuse your mind to such an extent that it cannot possibly do its job in an efficient way. Do you understand the impact that we are talking about?

The mind is in effect, a prisoner of your thoughts; it has lost its ability to function at its peak. In essence, it is like someone coming in and saying "I will do your job for you" even though they are not trained in this field of work. This is what we are doing with our minds. It is fully aware of what to do if left in peace.

Now enter thoughts and emotions run wild. This creates a whole mess of things. The mind can no longer operate on the level it is meant to. Its job has now become dodging and struggling against an onslaught of thoughts that are clouding the mind. This is not its job; its only function is to clearly and peacefully connect with its innate wisdom to bring through knowledge already in place. While it fights and struggles with too many thoughts, it is blocked from doing its job. The whole concept is quite simple really; just slow down the thought process and realize that you can leave the thinking up to the mind that is fully qualified for the job.

You, on the other hand, are just there to monitor the process and keep the negativity in check. That is your job. Thoughts have become so desensitized that most are not even aware of what is going on in their mind at all. When the mind becomes clouded, so does the judgment of the thinker. All that is required is a regular clearing out of the thoughts to reveal an already perfect system in place. You see, you were created with the innate ability to "know" the answers to all your questions and to live in a continuous state of peace and harmony. With all this 'dis-ease' in the mind there can be no real peace.

Open up your mind to see that all it takes is a complete letting go of the external events that are happening around you. This relieves you of the burden of doing something about it. Detachment is key here. Remain in a state of peaceful acceptance of your present circumstances and just know that you are cared for.

Struggling against the flow of events of your life only blocks the energy flow. Be accepting of who you are and your role in life. Love yourself and allow for an understanding to develop of who you are and why you are here. There are no mistakes, dear ones. Your roles have been hand-picked by yourselves for your unique learning needs. Having said this, why not create the very best possible situation for yourselves?

All that is required by you is your self-acceptance, self-love and a continual stream of positive thoughts in place of the negative. Things will simply fall into place all by themselves once you get this down pat. Life with all of its challenges need not be so difficult after all. Once you become aware of what your "job" is and what can be left up to the mind to accomplish, you are home-free.

Allow now, for this to sink in for a moment. This way of thinking requires a change of the way you see things. Let things come to you in a form of ultimate trust. You are relieved of the burden now of over-analyzing and feeling responsible to make things happen. If you stay out of your own way, things will happen as they were meant to. Realize that you are in control of your life and your destiny.

Things happen not by chance but in accordance to what the mind holds. This is why it is so very important that you gain control over what the mind is thinking. You in fact are the thinker of those thoughts with the mind to follow your lead, not the other way around. Relieve yourself of the burden of trying to over-think and "find" the answer to your question. Release the attachment to the problem and let the answer find you. You will see the simplicity with which this process works. And best of all, you are no longer in charge of every problem, decision, etc. You are flowing freely and standing out of the way of the capability of the mind to bring you the information you are looking for.

ALLOW THE BEST TO FLOW TO YOU

"Never give up on knowing that there is an easier way; only you can allow for the best to flow to you. Always start fresh with a positive, clean attitude and know that your life does make a difference and affects others. Welcome the intuitive nudges you receive and be in gratitude"

-Annett's Guides

◆ CHAPTER 7 ◆

MIGHTY I AM PRESENCE

On the outside it feels as though there is no end to the ever-increasing stream of thoughts. However, in reality, my dear friends, it is you who create each and every thought. Much of it stems from fear, worry, doubt and not being in the moment. Now, let us begin to paint another picture, shall we? This time, picture that at your fingertips you have the power to control what comes in and what goes out of your mind. This is indeed fact, however, unrealized by most. Begin to change how you think by increasing the positivity that is a part of your everyday reality.

This is really not as difficult as most of you may think…. just reach into your thoughts every so often and filter through to purify what stays. A few mere seconds each day with this method and you can change your entire reality. Yes, this is truth. Once you realize the depth that you can reach with this method you will be very excited indeed. With each passing day you will be creating, with your positive thinking, the reality that you so desperately seek. The idea here is to release yourself from the negative aspects that bind you so.

It is our sincere wish that each and every one of you masters this task this time around. This is the big chance to overcome what is holding you back from achieving your greatness. It is your destiny to far surpass all that you could possibly imagine or hope for in this lifetime. Why not give this method a go then? The only other alternative is to remain in a state of over-thinking, worrying and needless fear. You see dear ones; the time is upon you where your every thought will reverberate out into the universe affecting multitudes of other existences and lives.

Make a pledge to yourself that you will maintain a state of positivity at all times regardless of what is happening around you. For you see, the truth is that what is happening around you is merely a drama for you to participate in. Now you can choose to take the chaotic route and be immersed IN the drama, or you can learn by observation. Observation is another fantastic tool for learning. When using the tool of observation you are choosing to step outside of the drama that is unfolding and pick up clues to "read between the lines" of what is really going on. Those who choose to become immersed in the drama of their lives will remain in the dark about what is really going on.

You see, the opportunity exists for everyone equally to be the peaceful observer and learn by watching the events around you. This requires detachment, dear ones. Detachment is something that happens when you have no attachment to the outcome of events. Simple really; let go of the controlling aspect that binds so many of you at this time in your lives.

We, in the higher realms, are very clear about who and what we are about. You see, we have mastered our thoughts and emotions; hence the name "Ascended Masters."

When you get clear about what is going on in your head, you will then get clear about what you are here to do. This process is really not that difficult; it is just that you were programmed to believe that life is difficult. This deep-seated belief keeps you from realizing your innate wisdom and greatness. When the time is right, there will come a great and mass opportunity for those of you who are ready to take a grand leap. This leap will catapult you out of your present state of reality.

Thought creates reality, right? So, it stands to reason if you moved beyond and out of your current limiting thought system, a new reality would be born. All that you see is indeed changeable. By this we mean what you think, you create and therefore when you change your thoughts, you change the reality you inhabit. Open yourself up to the possibility that you are on a course to change. You can no longer avoid it. You current state of living is losing its edge. This way of being can only hold its own for so long, and then it is time to say "Wait a minute, I am not feeling satisfied here – there must be something more." You are right; there is something more and you have a way to access it.

Inside of each and every one of you resides a knowing of who you are and why you are here. There is indeed a Master Plan in effect and in short order you will become more aware of how you fit into this Master Plan. All those of you on Earth at this time came to participate in the "grand event" shall we say? When you took on this life you knew it would not be one of those mediocre ones, you knew you would be going out with a big bang. Suffice it to say, dear ones, you are en-route to your destiny with your Higher Selves.

By this we mean you are beginning, even as we speak, to wake up to the knowledge that you hold the keys within you to all you seek. By acknowledging this, you have taken the first step. Do not give your power away to another. They do not have authority over you; only YOU do. Be in your power at all times, dear friends. This is the way to reach your highest potential or best possible outcome for yourself.

Be in touch with your heart centers. This is the route to the higher realms. The love frequency holds the pattern of opportunity for transformation. Indeed, there is much strife on the Earth at this time; however the way to transcend and transform it is LOVE. Energy is transformable is it not? Then it stands to reason that the dark energies that reside on your planet can be transformed into light.

Now is the time, dear friends, to take matters into your own hands and change the way things are done. Old methods no longer work the way they did. As new information comes to you, be courageous and willing to step out of the norm. The norm by the way, is not really that 'normal' at all.

To experience and then re-experience a continual stream of negativity is merely habit, not a normal way of being. In fact, your normal state of being is one of tranquility and complete trust and knowing that you are cared for. With your intuition in check and an understanding that you are in charge here, you are well-equipped to step into your new life. And it is just that, a NEW life!

You see, your old way of being had a way of controlling you into believing that you are not the Master of your life. The thought process, if not held in check, can do this to you. Imagine now, if you will, a presence; this presence is your Higher Self or "Mighty I AM presence". This is the highest part of you – the all-knowing part. And, we all have one. You might be thinking, "Well that might be for some people, but I am not good enough for that kind of thing." Well, let me tell you directly from someone who knows; you ARE good enough and you DO have a mighty I AM presence!

When you begin to access this presence and acknowledge that it exists, it can and will assist you in your daily life. You see, it was never meant to play a back seat to the ego. The ego wants complete control over your life and just never lets up. What we mean here is that the higher all-knowing part of you is lying dormant until you acknowledge its presence. You see, there was a time when the Higher Self was in charge of the direction and goings on in your life.

And then it became outmoded. It was not the fashion to be all-powerful and KNOW with full authority and certainty who you are and what you are to do. Well, I have news for you; it is back in fashion NOW! Trust that you are being guided to your life's purpose with each new step that is being shown you.

This does not have to be a difficult process at all. You see, as you require the next piece of the puzzle, it appears. All that is required here is a little faith and trust that you are cared for and that there is a perfect system already in place.

Realize that all it takes is a letting go of the old way of doing things. This "old way" has taken dominion over your life long enough. Be in the clear by opening up to a new way of being. This new way, is in fact much easier and less taxing on the system. Your trust in the flow of events to take place as they will, while remaining detached, will activate this new way of being. All the while decipher what you will and will not let into your place of power: the mind!

YOUR INNER SELF

"Keep clear; stay connected to your "inner self." Life is not a "battle" to be won; but an opportunity to connect within and stay true to yourself. You will know you are connected from within when you do not feel a sense of urgency about life and a need to control the outcome. The guidance is always there; ask and you will receive the answer."

-Annett's Guides

◆ CHAPTER 8 ◆

YOU ARE THE FILTER

My dear friends, it is time for you to allow power and dominion over yourselves and your lives. The key way to accomplish this is to be in control of your thoughts. When you go about your daily business, stop and be aware of what comes and goes in your mind. Although this seems like an overly simplistic ritual, it is far from it.

This one small step can transform your whole life. Indeed, it can open up a whole new world for you! You see, dear ones, as you exist now, you are mostly controlled day in and day out by your constant chattering mind. This is, in effect, very debilitating.

Over the course of time, you become disconnected from the essence of your true selves. When you begin to master what comes in and out of your mind, you are then becoming aware of the very life that flows through you. This life or energy (life force, perhaps) is the essence of who you truly are. In your current state and undertakings of your existence you are a slave to your thoughts. This is highly unnecessary.

My friends think of it this way: when your thoughts are out of control you begin to walk in automatic pilot. This is not good (understatement). You see, when walking in this mode you are not even truly aware of your surroundings. By this we mean that your mind is clouded with "over-thinking" and in this way you are blocked from your inner guidance. This inner guidance is given to everyone as a means to navigate through the storms of life. This gift is highly under-used.

When the mind is so filled with unnecessary worry, fear, judgment etc., etc. the positive energy of the essence of who you are is unable to flow freely.

Try to imagine that you are a cylinder where energy is meant to flow freely. Now, imagine that the excess negative thoughts that you think are like heavy dirt that clogs the flow of energy. You were meant to be an "empty" container, so to speak. By this we mean only the positive is meant to stay and all else goes.

When you do this type of clearing on a regular basis, you will find that things in your life flow freely and without effort on your part. You say, "How is this possible?" I must suffer and work and try endlessly to control the events in my life so that they will stay in line." We say this to you: Hogwash! You have been sold a faulty bill of goods to believe in this way of thinking.

As we have said before, you are the Master and with this awareness, you say what goes in your life. If you say that you will take the easy route and allow things to fall into place for you, then that is exactly what they will do. Have we made ourselves clear on this subject yet? We realize you have a lot of "clogged" thinking going on and may have trouble taking this message into your brain.

We wish, above all else, to make this one point abundantly clear to all of you. Give up trying to be in control of your life. This is, in fact, illusion anyway. Allow the greater power that IS to guide your life for you. This is a much smoother, easier route to take, and in your heart you will recognize this path as familiar once you step onto it. As it sits now, you walk the bumpy, hazardous path. This path has no clear direction to it and makes things very difficult indeed. Why not take the other path?

We will pass on one other tidbit of information to you; by allowing things to come your way, you have given yourself an opportunity to watch for the "signs". On an ongoing and continuous basis, there are signs pointing out the way for you to walk.

These signs will have a way of guiding you to your life's purpose if you let them. Most of you are completely unaware of these signs, synchronicities and coincidences (whatever you want to call them). They are there for a purpose. When you become aware of and watch for these signs, they will show you the way.

Things will become ever clearer for you on your journey through life. However, until you begin to slow down the thought process, you will likely be unaware of most of the signs. They are all around at all times. They will point out the ultimate route for you to take for your highest good at any given time. There are usually three paths that you can take:

1) **The path of least resistance: the one that we recommend**
2) **The path that most of you follow: the one that has no direction**
3) **The destructive route: the one filled with negativity continuously**

Each time you think a thought, you are walking down one of these three paths. On a regular and continuous basis you are creating, with your thoughts, the reality that you live in. We mean this literally, not as a figure of speech as some of you may like to believe. Yes, your thoughts are this imperative to the quality of your life. Choose the path of least resistance, my friends; this is the quickest route to get to where you want to be.

Every soul that is incarnated on the Earth plane desires to be loved, accepted and valued. When you begin to walk the path of least resistance you will come across all of these things on a regular basis, as they will be coming from within yourself. That is where all the true power comes from: within. We encourage you, dear ones; make it easy on yourselves by choosing the easier path.

Until now, most of you have been holding the ingrained belief that to succeed and to find happiness, you must suffer for it bitterly. This is not truth and, as fiction, it is creating havoc in your lives only because you believe it is so. Remember my words: relieve yourself of the burden of attempting to "make things happen" in a certain way. If you step out of your own way you will begin to see a clear path ahead, the path of least resistance. Walking this path requires the least amount of effort; however the most amount of trust in where you are going.

As you begin to trust more and more in this "effortless" journey you will think, "Low and behold, I see a pattern developing here." You see, all it takes is an acceptance of who you are and what you are about. Simple. End of story.

By fighting to overcome and change the things you cannot change, you are, in fact, creating more difficulty for yourself. **All things that happen in your lives happen for a very specific reason. Indeed happen at exactly the right time, in the right way, and with the right people. There are no accidents and, if you choose to, you can always come out with the highest possible advantage by not resisting your current circumstances**.

When you begin to let go and recognize the possibility that the things you need and want will come to you, BINGO! You have begun to play the game the way it is meant to be played.

We, in the higher realms, never second guess the events in our lives. If it is in your face, then it is meant for you as a lesson to learn something very specific. You can do one of two things at this point: resist it and make it bigger and more menacing, or go with the flow and be accepting of it.

When you are accepting of a challenge that has come to you, you will move through it much more quickly than if you fight against it. The lessons that you need to learn require that you are open to an understanding of why they have come to you. Please begin to ask yourselves on a regular basis, "What do I need to learn here? What is it about this specific situation that brings me difficulty, and why?" These are key questions, dear ones, and questions that will bring you much power and understanding if you ask them on a regular basis.

When you allow events to unfold as they will, you will be quite surprised at the results of your efforts not to control the situation. As you will see, the knowledge and information that you need will come to you at just the right time. This is fact and we dare you to try it! We need to dare you at this point because we know that for most of you this would be an amazing feat to accomplish indeed. To most of you, the thought of not attempting to control your surroundings and the events in your life would be quite unthinkable. Try to think of it this way: Haven't you been through the wringer enough? Aren't you ready for a change? Indeed, we believe you are, so why not begin to try to see things in a different light? When you allow yourself to see things in a way that is more clear to you, you are already one step ahead of the game.

Life can be thought of as a game in the sense that once you recognize that you are meant to take the path of least resistance, you see that you can experience joy, ease and happiness on a regular basis instead of creating turmoil and suffering for yourselves. You see, as you let go of the negativity that surrounds you, you will then begin creating positivity on all levels for yourselves, beginning with the mental (thoughts) and then manifesting into your physical reality!

THE TRUTH WILL REVEAL ITSELF

"Trust your heart and instincts. The truth will reveal itself to you. Be not concerned with small details; live a life of joy, gratitude and clarity."

-Annett's Guides

◆ CHAPTER 9 ◆

DIVINE KNOWLEDGE

Dear ones, let us begin again today with a fresh start. That is what is required of you each day (each moment actually). You see the mind is quite a sponge or container, if you will, that gathers and holds information. The information is sometimes good, sometimes not so good. This "container" of yours needs emptying out on a regular basis. If you do so, you will begin to see major changes in your life. When the mind is clear, it has the ability to hold not only everyday knowledge but also information of a different sort altogether. What we are speaking of here is Divine knowledge (knowledge of the light, so to speak).

This higher knowledge is the answer to what you seek. Many of you on the Earth at this time crave a peace and tranquility that is just nowhere to be found. That is because it comes from inside yourselves. The truth and power comes from within. Truly, that is where you need to begin looking, not outside yourself. Empty your "container" regularly, dear ones.

For at this time, it is filled with much that is not even your own. By this we mean you are a receptacle that can be used as a dumping ground for other people's stuff. When you take on another's issues or negativity, then you begin to become overloaded in the sense that your container is overflowing with a heaviness that weighs you down severely. Please be conscious in your daily undertakings, be aware that your mind, and how you go about using it is so very important. It can be used in a most powerful manner if you allow it to be so. You see, (and I will continue to repeat my message as often as necessary), on this journey that you call life, you have tests and you have trials put before you to teach you lessons. The way to pass the test is to be conscious in every moment of your reality of NOW. Your NOW has extreme power and the potential to create whatever it is that you desire.

Yes, this is truth, dear ones. As you are so overloaded in your minds and as you choose negativity over positivity, you are indeed blocking this God-given gift of manifestation.

Now imagine if you will, a garden: one that is flourishing with life and abundantly full. Now the opposite – one that is dying off in every way – dried up with no life in it. What is the difference? The first is flourishing because it has the life-force of sunshine and water to nourish it. And so it is with the mind; the "sunshine and water" are positivity and clear-mindedness. We cannot emphasize enough the importance of a clear mind, dear ones.

As you go about your daily business, continue to peek inside to see what is dwelling in your power centre: your mind. We wish it to be known to you, here and now, that anything your heart desires can come through the power of the mind. We do understand that it has become a most difficult process, this clearing of the mind in the midst of all the chaotic energies that surround your planet Earth. Nevertheless, please be the exception; do it on a daily basis.

Recognize that you are Masters in your own right; only the continued density of your planet has made it more and more difficult to reach for the light. However, be aware that with your intention you can do it! All it takes is your intention to create the life you desire through your positive thoughts.

And, so you say, yes, but my situation is a lost cause; I cannot possibly change it now." We say this to you: inside of yourself sits a seed that if you watered, nourished and cared for it will grow. What we are trying to say is: what you focus on grows and takes precedence in your life. Although you have many obstacles put before you that you must learn to work around or with, so to speak, do not despair. You still have every ability and every opportunity to seek out the light. This light is all around you and can show you the way to your highest potential at any given time.

Now, we hope that we are beginning to make ourselves very clear to you at this point. Dwelling on the negative aspects of one's life only emphasizes those aspects and continues to draw to you more of the same. Like attracts like, you see? Why not then, on a continuous basis, attract to you that which you desire? We know you may say this sounds much too simple and too good to be true, but know that it is every bit truth and then some!

The real tragedy here is that you have been sold a bill of goods that says the opposite. And for the most part, you have bought into it hook, line and sinker. You see, there are those who are not of the light that do not have your best interest at heart. These beings, so to speak, would have you stay in the dark regarding your unlimited power and ability. To break the mold, you must begin to see things in a much more expanded way. By opening up your awareness, you can begin to examine your surroundings with the clear intention that you will read between the lines.

What we are saying is that once you begin to search for the truth and the real meaning behind any given situation, you will begin to learn and grow. In order to do so, you need to give up a few things: negativity, dependency, worry, fear, control and other emotions of this nature. When you choose to begin to see things with your higher awareness or consciousness, you need to remain in a state of objectivity. In order to do this, the negative thoughts, emotions and behaviors must go. We cannot emphasize this point enough! Generally speaking, most negative emotions, thoughts, etc, are born out of fear stemming from low self-esteem, inferiority, etc.

Once you begin to realize that as a soul you are perfect as is (no need for repair or exchange) then you can begin to accept and love yourself for who you are. You see, once again we will refer to the media and those in a position of 'power'. These types see things from a 'money-money' point of view and therefore will do anything necessary to continue to keep people in the dark regarding their inborn, innate wisdom and potential.

Each and every one of you has the potential to strive toward the light and change your life. It is not necessary to be rich, famous, etc. All that is required is your intention to create the best life for yourself that you can, with the resources you have, to become the soul you were meant to be. Regardless of race, creed, wealth, living conditions, and so on. You have the choice of which path you will walk. Will it be the path that serves not the Creator but the negativity and dark influences, or will it be the Light? Yes, all this can be achieved through your perspective and your thoughts. As you remain in positivity with the pure intent to 'love thy neighbor' and be of service to others, you are serving the light and it grows stronger. As you choose the path of negativity, an "eye for an eye" for example, you service the dark and it becomes stronger. The choice is yours. So important is the mind and what you choose to do with it.

Just as important is the heart centre and what you choose to do with it. Do you choose to hold onto hurt and anger and resentment, or do you choose to forgive, heal and move toward the light once again?

As you come to Earth, you always have free will to choose to your liking. What you do with your time allotted to you will be the deciding factor as to what you will be able to accomplish in the realms of light. Life, of course, is eternal and continues on even after 'till death do us part'. This separation is only temporary at best and there is always a reunion of loved ones on 'the other side', as you like to call it.

We, the hierarchy of Ascended Masters feel most honored to be helping in this way, through this book. We know the path is not easy when you choose to incarnate on the Earth; however, you also realize the great opportunity set before you at this time, dear ones. Never lose sight of it.

The potential for spiritual liberation is great, this time period is most precious. Be always on the lookout for ways to better yourself and your life. You see, each and every event, word, behavior, etc.is duly recorded and not lost. And thus, you are responsible for yourself in a very big way. Each kind or unkind deed is tallied and kept track of. When you pass over in spirit you will be made aware of where you stand on the spiritual ladder of success. How well do you think you will have done when it is all said and done?

We implore you to think on these things ahead of the game. And life can truly be a delightful game when you attempt to be the best you can and are lending a helping hand to others. Kind deeds rate very highly on the 'other side' and money counts for naught. So there you have it folks, today's lesson in a nutshell, made simple and straightforward for all to understand and contemplate on. There are many of us on your side to support you through your life trials, so do not despair; you are never alone. When you strive to reach the light, the entire Kingdom of Heaven opens itself up to you!

THE INNER REFLECTS THE OUTER

"Have fun, play, sing, dance, and move; don't allow your 'emotional' energy to become congested. Then, your physical body will not become congested. Go easy on yourself; the inner reflects the outer! Sometimes the problem is necessary for a time (like a blankie); don't be concerned and trust in the perfect timing for releasing it!"

-Annett's Guides

◆ CHAPTER 10 ◆

THE POWER OF IMAGINATION

I am the Master Kuthumi once again at your service. I have been trying to impart to you the message of the power of the mind and consequently, your thoughts and thinking process. In the ideal, one would have a clear mind except for that which is happening in the moment and requires our direct interaction, so to speak. All else is unimportant, you see, the amount of time and energy directed towards that which is not in the "NOW" is truly a waste of your valuable brain power.

I speak to you from a higher perspective and know what I am talking about. Whenever you give your energy to a past or a future thought, you are missing out on the power of NOW. The power of NOW is so very important that if all you did was put your energy towards it, you would truly be a master- piece in the making.

We do understand that once you begin to get pulled down into the whirlwind of thoughtlessness – not really being aware of what goes on in there (your mind), it is indeed quite a task to pull out of it. However, please remember, with each passing moment, you DO indeed have what it takes to draw yourself out of the vortex and into the flow of positive creativity. Positive creativity is a place in which you begin to manifest your life and what you choose to create in it. The idea that you are helpless and simply exist to take whatever comes your way is an outmoded way of thinking!

Please, on a regular basis, continue to clear out all negative or excess thoughts from your mind; this has the effect of a strainer clearing out impurities. You see, the impurities act as barriers: barriers to your health, barriers to your ability to create the life you desire. Now, all of you have your dreams, so to speak, well I say GET ON WITH IT! It is not nearly as difficult as you think it may be. By choosing the positive over negative you are one step closer to realizing and creating your dream(s)!

In all ways, the path continues to move back towards the thoughts and thinking process. You see, at one time it was common place to have complete control of the mind; it was used as the tool it was intended for.

Now, there are indeed so very many distractions and challenges in today's world that it has become quite a task to filter out the 'impurities'. Please consider this for a moment my friends: your mind is so incredibly powerful that it is possible to literally create an entire world from it!

Let me elaborate, there is much in existence that you are not aware of, that you cannot see, and so it stems to reason that there is in existence a whole array of possibilities and creations that are not of this world.

Also, please understand that the mind holds unlimited capacity. By this we mean, where you believe there to be limitation, there is in fact none. The pressures of daily living on this planet you call Earth can 'suck the life right out of you' to use one of your expressions, (but only if you let it). This energy sucking process is due in large part to the misuse of the mind, your amazing creating tool.

At this time I would like to introduce to you the power of imagination. With this powerful tool you may create to your heart's content. Seems like a fairytale you say? **Well, we have news for you: what you can visualize or imagine, you can create.** Let me spell this out for you in greater detail (since your imagination may have been accustomed to being stifled). As the thought is akin to a living, breathing organism, the energy that you put into motion by thinking about something, begins to attract to you the very thing you are thinking about. "Wait a minute you say, I do not see how that can possibly work." When you begin to be more aware of what goes on inside your head on an ongoing basis, then you will begin to make the connection.

As it sits now for most of you, you do not have even the foggiest idea of what goes on in there because it is so clouded with over-thinking! In this lesson of learning to tame the mind, there begins a ripple effect of peace, serenity, clarity and an abundance of creating the positive in your life. If you leave the mind to be as a wild lion, then it is out of control and you are unable to sustain proper concentration for any length of time.

So then, let us review the lessons for today: on the outside there are many distractions and can pull you from your true life's purpose in a flash. On the inside, lies the power of the mind, a power to be reckoned with if I do say so myself. When you are able to harness the amazing power of the mind, the thoughts begin to create a life of their own (one that you wish for yourself).

In these times of incredible uncertainty, we, the Ascended Masters say to you: be ever on the lookout for this pervasive negativity; it can and will permeate your every waking moment if you let it. It is everywhere; in the Media, on the streets and in an ever-growing 'pollution' surrounding the energy-field of planet Earth. This type of pollution is far worse and far more damaging than the kind you can see hovering in your air. For once the thought-field is polluted; it takes a massive effort on your part to clean this act up. When you have an accumulation of negative thought-forms that are beginning to build up, then we say to you, "look out, you are in for quite a ride!" This thought-form then begins to carry on with a life of its own.

We mean here that, as we have said, thoughts are a living energy affecting all around it and hence, it begins to carry with it the ferocity of a very large, wild, rabid animal. This animal begins to create others of its kind and presto, they are off and running with fear and negativity as their food to keep them alive! These animals or negative thought-forms if you will can perpetuate a great deal of damage to all who reside on the Earth. For as we have said, the worst kind of pollution is the thought-form kind.

On the other hand, as you begin to move into continual positivity and become thought-aware, you can begin to clean up this mess! I am ready to bring a new awareness to all who will have the ears to hear me. When one is ready to listen, they are ready to make changes in their life.

I am the Master Kuthumi and my specialty is one of opening up the mind. What I mean here, is that many of you have clogged channels in the mind. These channels are filled up with negative thoughts. When you become aware of them, you can begin releasing them. When this happens you then have new channels of awareness that can then be used for positivity. In this way, you have a whole new array of channels that can be filled with energy or thoughts, which can be programmed for your personal use.

You see, as it sits now, the mind is filled with useless and often destructive thoughts that only serve to hinder you at every turn. If you choose to open up these channels and clear them out, you will have much more space, if you will, to use for your highest good. There is a very low percentage of the brain's full capacity being used by most today. You can harness a much higher percent by being AWARE of what goes on in the mind. Those on the Earth at this time have become so desensitized to what goes on in the mind, that they are not even aware of their own thoughts. You wonder, "How could that be?" "We are not even aware of our own thoughts?" And we say, "Yes, it is true." Now once we are in agreement of that one point (and it is a big one), then perhaps we can make some headway! Yes? Okay then.

Remember how I have been explaining to you all that you can create your own life by choosing what you think? Well, I wish that you would take that literally. You see, we live in the times where uncertainty has become the name of the game. Being as many of you cannot even keep track of what goes on in the mind; it stands to reason that it is difficult to believe that what you think, you create! To make this even clearer, let me give an example: as you are going about your busy day, and scarcely have time to even take a breath, your mind is wandering all over the place on an ongoing basis. With this type of thinking you cannot possibly have a controlled mind, and therefore, a life that you are in control of. Please begin to make it a regular habit in your life, to tap into your thoughts and be the filter for your mind.

GETTING TO KNOW YOURSELF

"Concentrate on getting to know yourself; certain parts want to be expressed; feel free to connect inside and just listen quietly. Whatever you desire is yours, whatever you wish to change or create new is yours. Don't hold on, or need to know all the answers. Be in the here and now, and you will see the grand outcome you envisioned for yourself coming to pass." -Annett's Guides

◆ CHAPTER 11 ◆

BEING YOUR AUTHENTIC SELF

You are crossing over a threshold now that will have you adjusting your eye lenses, so to speak. The vision which you choose for yourself is the one that will unfold for you. Be very careful how you construct your thoughts and which desires you 'put out there'. In this accelerated time of energetic flow, what you put out comes back magnified at a very fast rate.

We say this to you: "Be the example for your children, for they only know that which you vibrationally pass onto them." That which you accept as truth, they will also accept as truth. Be true in your heart to yourself, so that which you create in your life is of the purest (the essence of your authentic self).

We know that you would wish for your children to be nothing but the best. The best is their true self, not a fabricated one, which society has imposed upon them. It is time to become all of who you are, not the version that you pretend to be, in order to be pleasing or acceptable to others. This will take some letting go on your parts. Delve deep within yourself to see what you might be holding onto in terms of this question: "Who do I think I am supposed to be?" By asking this question, dear hearts, you might be surprised at what you find lurking within the shadows of your heart.

Your reality can become quite different when you begin shedding the old layers of 'clothing'. These cloaks have been designed by you to distract yourselves from your true authentic self. There needs to be a 'coming out party,' so to speak. At this party, you are the star of the show and must be willing to release the parts of you that are the impostors. The degree to which you can 'come out' of yourself is the degree to which your children will be free to also come out and become their authentic self.

By design, you were meant to be individuals of uniqueness and individuality. Society dictates more of a 'clone' mentality one in which you follow the leader blindly. The originality and true spark is then missing. Adjust your way of thinking so that when you share your thoughts with your loved ones you are in alignment with your original self Judging yourself only serves to block your true creativity and essence of Self. The true self likes to come out and play when all restrictions are removed and it is honored. This path of choice will serve you well once you become accustomed to trusting your Higher Self to guide your thoughts and actions. By this we mean, focus on sharing from the heart what feels like truth to you, not what will feed the status quo. Those who are in true alignment will be of greater service to themselves and all those around them.

You are indeed, never alone and so powerful is the connection of light beings that surround you in your everyday living experience. Know that by being the true light that you are, you shine brightly for those that look up to you (namely, your children). Being a fully connected human being is what it is all about! If you are disconnected from your true self and self-expression, they too will follow suit. You indeed have a great responsibility as a parent to allow yourself full expression of your true self with the idea that the children will also enjoy the same freedom. There is no greater freedom than that of true self expression from the heart. Not an expression of thoughts and ideas based on negative beliefs about yourself that are not even true!

Now is the time to fully delve into the truth of who you really are. By letting go of old patterns, you will easily begin to come into alignment with your true nature and have a better understanding of what you will be able to accomplish in this lifetime.

As you continue to let go of old, out-dated, and negative patterns of thought and action you will become aware that your new self is beginning to peek through. Clouded-thinking is quite common when operating from a level of "What can I do to please you and be accepted?" Dear ones, keep this foremost in your mind at all times, whenever you are interacting with others. This way of being will only serve to stifle the authentic and original self that is in alignment with your highest good. Be in a continuous state of allowing the true essence of you to come to the forefront. It is not nearly as difficult as you might think.

Your self-expression is a natural thing, simply put: it has been squashed by opinions, thoughts and ideas of others. When you allow the full expression to shine through you, you will notice that others are drawn to you like bees to honey. The reason for this is that they are drawn to that which is truth and authenticity, knowing intuitively that this will also empower them.

Draw the line, then, on how you choose to interact with others from this point forward. Will it be from your ego, which is fear-based and 'controlling' your ability to be a free-flowing individual? Or, will it be from a place of freely allowing your true nature to shine through? We would encourage the latter, as that is what will bring you the most joy and satisfaction in your daily living experience. It can and will become quite effortless if you choose it to be so. Simply loosen up the reins on your self-judgment, self-criticism and the need to be accepted. Acceptance will come automatically (from yourself and others) when you are in alignment with your true self. Begin to see yourself as you are seen from the higher realms: a fully intact being that is on a journey back to their original self.

The opportunity to connect or more precisely 'reconnect' is available at all times for you to take advantage of. There will be times when it feels so much more comfortable to simply remain 'in the box' as they say, by continuing the old pattern of 'people-pleasing'. This is due to the fact that your energy-frequency that you vibrate on is set at a certain level in the old pattern or paradigm. Once you begin to shift your vibration to a new level, it can quite literally knock you off balance! As you shift your vibration, you are atom for atom becoming a new person at the cellular level. Sometimes this can cause you to feel like you are coming undone (unraveling like a knitted sweater!).

As you practice patience and diligence you will become more comfortable in your new 'body' that now has shifted to a different energy-pattern (frequency). As you move forward (sometimes back and forth) from the old frequency to the new, you will find yourself more and more feeling at home in the new reality. It does require effort on your part, as the temptation to remain in familiar territory is greater than the desire to move ahead at first. Feeling comfortable is often the order of the day, rather than feeling out of sorts to create change. Know that by allowing yourself to feel uncomfortable you will be taking a step in the right direction with the goal of being the true self.

You see, everyone has been given a navigational tool to know when they are connected as their true self and when they are not. When the connection is weakening, the result is a feeling of "pressure to perform". This pressure to perform is an indicator that you have slipped off the track and are now operating based on what is expected by others, not what feels authentic to you. Each and every time you choose to be authentic to you, you have created a deeper groove in which to walk next time. It will be easier to find and easier to walk this pathway. Each and every time you ignore your intuitive nudges to go this way, do this, say this, don't do that, you dig a deeper hole for yourself in terms of losing your true nature.

We say this to you: "Be ever aware of what you true nature would like to express. This is a simple matter of being in the moment and connecting to what is occurring within. What is occurring within will be the indicator or gauge of what needs to be looked at, talked about, felt, or in whatever way acknowledged and accepted.

Trouble occurs when one denies the inner connection and begins to follow the crowd. Many are walking the path most travelled, rather than the path of least resistance. The path of least resistance is always the easiest path for you to take, that brings the most joy, creates the most satisfaction and allows for full expression of who you are.

SHIFTING FREQUENCIES

Simply by allowing your true nature to express itself, you have a sure-fire formula for staying connected to your inner source of power. This inner source of power will play itself out through you in such a way that will benefit not only yourself but everyone you come into contact with. When coming from this source of empowerment, you are coming from the highest level of 'you' possible.

Trust that if you allow yourself to 'come out' you will be in the right place at the right time and your life will have an effortless flow to it. Accept and know the fact that when you bring forward that which is within you, and begin to share it with others, the burden of life lifts and is replaced with joy. When you have a sense of peace emanating from you, you know you are connected to your true essence of Self. You will always be taking a step in the right direction when you trust, allow, and let go of struggling against the current of whatever is occurring for you in the moment.

We, in the higher realms will support you in whatever way we can by uplifting your thoughts, emotions and energy to a level that will inspire and help you move forward. All of you are being adjusted daily, on an energy level to support your spiritual growth. Every effort made by you to move into higher levels by focusing on your thoughts will be rewarded in the most empowering way. Truly, the work is done from the inside out, and when you have that in order all else falls into place effortlessly.

Many of you wish to create changes in your life and feel stuck in the groove of the old patterns. There is always time and methods to free you from your own self-imprisoned realities. Remain awake and alert to what is coming to you, for the answer to your question and/or problem is always trying to find its way to you! You are simply allowing yourself to put blinders on and not receiving the information given to you due to fear of change. By allowing the guidance to flow to you, you will see that your situation is not nearly as dire as you may have thought. Many of you believe that it has been too long, the situation is too challenging and there simply is no way out for you. We would wholeheartedly disagree with you there. There is never a better time than right now, this moment. to begin to re-create your life. You have all the tools, abilities and resources to do so. This is guaranteed; as no one takes on an earthly life without everything they need to fulfill their purpose to the highest level without everything they need from within them.

So, if you are feeling trapped by life's circumstances and feel that there is no way out, look again. Begin to question your possible motives as to why you may be holding onto your specific situation or circumstances. We guarantee you, you will see that a part of you is responsible in a big way for where you are. Beginning to accept responsibility for having created your situation in the first place will be the stepping stone to re-creating something new for yourself.

As long as you pass the buck onto the next guy and play the blame game, you will remain in the situation until you clearly find why you have created the situation in the first place. What do you need to learn here? When this becomes clear to you, you will be free to move onward and upward. We say to you: become very aware of why you do things, this will give you the key to letting go of the old you.

Know that by letting go of the old you, you will be making way for a better version of yourself. This does take some courage on your part, as by letting go of the old, you will, for a time, remain in unknown territory so to speak. Residing in this unknown territory can be an uncomfortable process, but a very necessary one in order for you to go through cleansing the old self. This purifying process has a way of wiping the slate clean so that you can begin to write a new script for your life. You are the creator of it and are free to design the very best life for yourself possible.

Understand that your path is not set in stone; there are varying experiences of life that you can choose from and still fulfill the original purpose and intent set out by your over-soul (higher self). We encourage you to dig deeper into yourself to see what lurks there in the way of fear or self-abandonment. By this we mean, where have you bailed on yourself when the going got tough? This self-analysis is necessary in that by coming to terms with what has happened in the past, you can rewrite your script for the future with a different outcome. This time, you will know what to avoid and what to focus on.

SHIFTING FREQUENCIES

Being keenly aware of what your strengths and weaknesses are will be of high value to you when going through this cleansing process. Many people never take the time to take inventory of themselves in such a way that will help them to create change and give them a leg up on who they truly are. Life need not be as difficult as most people make it. They are simply conditioned to believe it to be difficult and therefore they create it for themselves!

Know that by joining forces with the highest level part of you, you are setting yourself up to come from a position of power and not feel powerless.

In this sense, you will know who you are, what you are about, where you are going and how to get there! Sounds like a simple plan, does it not? Well, we assure you, that by operating from the level of authenticity this will happen automatically for you! Trust your instincts to guide you on this matter. The heart knows what it likes, how it wants to be and what is best for you. Continually consult with the heart where matters of your life are concerned and you will come out the winner. Your heart will also keep you 'safe' so to speak. What we mean here is that by following the internal nudges of the heart, you will always be in the right place at the right time and find that your life has the most amazing flow to it!

Rather than forcing yourself to do what you 'should' do in the moment, try going with the flow. You will find that by trusting what feels right in the moment, you will indeed have the best outcome for you at any given time. Trust, allow, trust and allow. Follow this pattern for the best possible outcome.

Take the time to know yourself. Many do not do this, and find that when they are alone, they have no clue of who they really are. Their perception of 'Self' is based on what others expect of them. Know that by taking the time to know yourself you are investing in the most priceless commodity around, yourself! There is nothing more important or more worthy of your time than this. Be willing to take a good, long hard look at yourself, the good, the bad and the 'ugly' so to speak, and realize that you are a package deal. You cannot separate the parts from each other, nor would you want to. This is what makes you, you and wholly unique unto yourself. Each part is necessary for you to be a whole individual, therefore it is best to allow for each part to be acknowledged and accepted without judgment or criticism. The more you are able to do this, the more you will find that your parts begin to transform into what you wish them to be!

As they are loved and accepted, they begin to relax, feel peaceful and then feel safe to transform themselves before your very eyes. And, by the same token, as you judge or criticize those parts that you deem 'unworthy', not good enough etc. they dig their heels in even farther and hold on for dear life!

Choose to be the ever-present guardian of your thoughts and feelings about yourself. Only you can choose to do this. Become aware of how you see yourself and how you perceive others see you. Question yourself anytime you have the urge to express an opinion that you know will agree with another, but is not fully your own. Be ever on the lookout for that pervasive people-pleasing part that will do anything to feel loved and accepted. Each and every time you give in to the urge to please at the expense of yourself, you, in essence, lose another piece of your power. Each and every time you express from the truth of who you are, you establish a framework of power source for yourself to draw from. You will begin to feel more whole as a person; feeling stable and grounded.

It is your choice in each moment to either come from truth or choose to come from a place of fear of rejection. We will give you a little tidbit of advice in this regard: connect within to your source of who you truly are and have a regular communication with it. As if speaking with a friend, ask your inner-self what it likes, where does it like to go, what does it like to do? In this way, you are strengthening the connection to your true authentic self and supporting yourself at a core level. This will serve you well in the times to come. The more well-acquainted you become with your inner-self now, the easier it will be to stay ever-present and connected when you are tested in the rough waters of life.

Justify to yourself, that when you take the time to allow yourself to be as and what you truly are, you are in a position of power. Working with what "god gave you" allows you to become more of who you are. By becoming more of who you are, you give others permission to do the same. This is key in terms of shifting to the new paradigm or new Earth. Allowing yourself to come out and shine will bring more positive results faster than any other route you can take.

The important part is to allow yourself to be in respect and acceptance of yourself as a whole being. No one was created perfect, but all have a perfect expression of themselves that will bring upliftment and connection to themselves and those around them. This connection is a link in a very long chain of souls that are coming from authenticity. This very vibration or energy field that is emitted from one who is connected to their authentic truth is a power to be reckoned with! Every time you choose to come from a viewpoint or position of what you truly believe, you are literally emitting a force field of light that brings purification to all around it. This purification allows for all that is not truth to dissolve and be replaced with pure source energy.

Simply by allowing yourself to express your true nature, will you be able to be of service to humankind by helping to purify the Earth with your energy field! Such is the importance of staying connected to what is truth for you. By letting go of others' expectations and pressure on you to be what they want you to be, you are well on your way to coming from a place of power, rather than disempowerment. It is all too common for the pattern to be one of, "I will just conform to fit in, and that way I won't cause any waves" mentality. Although this may not "cause any waves" it will also bind you to a life of mediocrity that will not nourish your soul and sense of well-being. Just go with the flow of who you are, remain in non-judgment of self, have a sense of fun about the whole thing and enjoy just being you! It really can be that simple, indeed, if you allow it to be so. By practicing this, you will begin to feel a sense of worthiness about yourself that you may never have felt before. Connection to worthiness comes from allowing yourself to be who you are without restriction.

You will begin to notice a pattern of self-acceptance forming once you are in the habit of just allowing yourself to be who you are without feeling the need to bend to another's will. Each and every time you forfeit your truth to bend to another's will you are sabotaging yourself in becoming more of who you are. Your sense of self will begin to diminish and you will begin to feel unworthy, when the truth is you are valuable beyond measure. In these times ahead, we implore you to begin to explore your true self, wants, desires and sense of self-expression, like you never have before. By doing so, you will be 'letting the cat out of the bag' so to speak, but in a good way. Once unleashed, the creativity that lies dormant within will begin to take on a life of its own and work in your favor.

Never under-estimate the power of creativity in its full expression of self; this power is the true you at the core level of your being and will create an expression of 'you'. Whenever you create from the core level of self, what is created will be of benefit to all who come into contact with it. Your creative energy will not create 'mistakes' because it is coming from the true source and from joy. By creating from within yourself, you will always produce something of value that is required at some level by someone or something. Trust that by letting go, connecting within, and allowing creativity loose, you will be a creator of a valuable commodity in whatever form it comes forth. We encourage you to wholeheartedly believe in yourself. Trust your intuition to guide you on your journey to connecting within. There is a divine path laid out for you that will bring you the most joy once you come from a place of trusting Self. Moment by moment, choice by choice and step by step you are the creator of your reality.

By understanding that you have already come such a long way in this very lifetime, you can choose to take yourself the rest of the way by taking it a step further! By this we mean, exploring internally until you find that connection or inner-link to all of the possibilities for yourself. This inner-link connection is where you will find the most inspiration, the most guidance and, when followed, the most peace and joy that your life could possibly contain.

Begin to daily, expect whatever it is that you desire to manifest itself into form in your reality, and you will see it beginning to take shape. Allow the best to find its way to you. And we truly do mean allow, because for many of you the good has a hard time finding its way to you because of your need to make things difficult. Enjoy this process of getting to know yourself, what you like, what you will accept into your life, and what you will not.

If you are willing to accept what another puts on you simply because you feel you could never get anything better, then that is exactly what you will have as your experience. Once you decide, "OK, enough is enough and I will no longer tolerate this situation" you will automatically begin to attract to yourself a new creation (experience).

The Universe knows no bounds (limitations) whatsoever, the only limitations are those created by your thoughts, expectations and beliefs about what you deserve. Begin to see yourself in a whole new light and celebrate the powerful being that you are! By doing so, you will begin to experience a whole new life. Know that you have every resource within you to begin to create these changes any time you so choose. The choosing part is important; you are the only one who can choose what type of reality or experience you will create for yourself.

By taking on a new attitude of "I deserve nothing but the best", you will begin to see that your life experience will reflect this way of thinking. Most definitely, you are the one playing your hand and unless you choose to let someone see your 'cards' and follow what they would have you do, remember that you are the ultimate authority and decision-maker in your life.

Far too often, we see souls giving away their power left, right and center to anyone who will alleviate the pressure of having to 'make that decision'. When you give away your power and authority in your life over to another who you feel is more qualified to know what is best for you, your life is now being designed according to another's blueprint! This blueprint or design will have another's signature and style on it. The outcome will be that you are following a pathway designed by another's dreams and desires. These desires may or may not have your best interest at heart.

The only sure-fire method of creating a blueprint or design that will fit you to a "t" would be for you to have the courage to create it from scratch yourself. You will see that the process can be quite exhilarating and fun once you get the hang of it. The first step is to let go of the notion that someone else has all the answers about you and your life/situation. By design, you were created to be the authority in your life and have the answers and solutions to every situation that could possibly arise, simply by listening to the small inner voice. This guidance will never steer you in the wrong direction. Simply by trusting your inner connection and allowing your life to unfold for you based on that guidance, you will have the best navigation system around. This process is fool-proof and one that needs to be used more by most of you with less merit put on other's opinions and ideas about you and your life! Accept that by doing so, you are coming into your own power more readily and will feel less at the mercy of another and their influence over you.

◆ CHAPTER 12 ◆

THE SOURCE OF ALL THAT IS

Now may we speak on the subject of control dramas? This topic may seem trivial or unimportant to you; however, I assure you it is most important. Many of you feel the pull to consciously or unconsciously draw energy from another; this is the way of your world. Although it feels natural to you, it is not. I will give you an example of what I am talking about; when a child is born, it is most likely born to parents who have not learned to draw energy from the source (God), whatever you call it, the name is not important. Now, when this happens, the habit of drawing energy from one another is formed. It is passed on from generation to generation and pretty soon you have an entire society who base their actions, thoughts, feelings etc. on how to manipulate others for their own gain. This destructive pattern is one that has to be stopped, for it is a lose-lose situation. This habit born out of necessity to survive is cultivated early on in life and therefore no other way of life is known.

This form of energy taking is so subtle and not even noticeable to most, however it is happening everywhere. Take for example, the fact that most of you are allowing another to draw from your energy source for their own gain. You, in fact, are allowing this transaction to take place, for somewhere in your consciousness it is an understood agreement between you and another party or parties. Please begin to allow yourself awareness that on another level much is taking place even beyond your knowledge. Begin to draw to you a shield of protection and the intent that you will no longer allow this to take place in your life. Once you have mastered the ability to draw energy directly from Source and not allow another to take from you, you have begun to play the game to win.

These forms of "control dramas" take the player of the game into a position where through manipulation, by use of emotion and intention; another is drawn into their drama. This form of energy-taking is depleting a person's supply and keeps them from experiencing their own innate power. The reservoir of energy I speak of, coming from Source, is of course, unlimited.

There is a mass belief that energy is in low supply and must be fought tooth and nail to attain. Why not try an experiment? Release your fears and imagine if you will a reservoir or channel of energy; this energy is unlimited and continuously flowing on an ongoing basis. Choose now to tap this channel of energy and allow it to flow through your body. As you do this you are tapping the unlimited supply directly from the Source of All That Is. Just the mere thought of it brings it to you and you may access it at any time you choose to do so.

We emphasize here CHOOSE to do so because many of you have been in despair so long that it has become unthinkable to be able to access something so simple, so pure and so completely healing. Never think that it is outside of yourself and not available to you. In fact, it is a part of you, only you have shut yourselves off from it! We emphasize once more the importance of choosing to connect with this all-pervading life-force. With your intention, much can be accomplished. As you put your attention on something its energy or influence begins to grow. Know that imagination and intention is more than mere fantasy. In fact through your imagination and intention you can bring to you that which you desire. Be still now and listen to your heart: what does it say? What is your heart trying to call to you?

If you continuously choose to look outside of yourself and to others for the answers you are continuing to miss the point! We know, it is easier to trust someone else's wisdom or ideas than your own. However, we must emphasize here; why trust someone else's beliefs over your own? As you begin to become still within yourself on a daily basis you will be amazed at how clear things become for you.

SHIFTING FREQUENCIES

Most are walking around in a haze where the slightest notion or belief of someone else's can sway them in a second. Take the time to calm the thoughts and quiet the mind. You will see that the perplexities of life will begin to become much less complex and your awareness of who you are and why you are here will begin to shine through! Please gauge your time carefully. Know what you are about and what your strengths and weaknesses are. By doing this, you are one step ahead of the game and ready to be a leader in times of mass change.

As you tap into the quiet within yourself you will begin to see a picture taking shape. This picture includes the informed and the uninformed. The informed are those who took the time to go within on a daily basis. These individuals are preparing for what is to come. They are aware on an entirely different level that big change is upon them, and all who reside on Mother Earth.

If we look at this from a different angle, perhaps we can make the picture a little bit clearer. When you continue to take in mental stimuli that surround and bombard your thinking process, you begin to run on overload. If you take the time to clear out this mental bombardment, you then have the ability to choose what stays and what goes. When you are bombarded on a regular basis, as you all are in your very overly-busy, hectic, chaotic lives, the mind can only hold so much. It then begins to operate on automatic pilot. This is not good. Automatic pilot suggests that someone else is in control and not the original recipient. BINGO! Have we gotten your attention now? We hope so, because we need you to begin to think on another level so that a higher capacity of the brain can be used.

Why do you think such a low percentage of the brain is currently being used by most on the planet? Overuse, over-thinking, and continuous intake with no time for downloading the thoughts and ideas that have accumulated over time. Please give this idea some serious thought. Consider this: many of you try to get out of situations that are less than ideal and find that it just cannot be done. This is due to the way that you think about it. The constant barrage of negative thoughts creates a barrier to the positive outcome you are trying to create for yourselves. What we mean here, quite literally, is if you would stop trying to fight the circumstance and simply allow (and expect) the best possible outcome, it would simply be attracted to you. This is the law of energy.

When you force the issue, you are blocking possible avenues or ways that the situation could be remedied, or drawing to you whatever it is you desire. Begin to try to observe the thought process every so often. More, than less often would be good. As you begin to do this, you will begin to notice a whole string of thoughts that began with one thought. This in turn begins a whole new line of thoughts. By beginning to tone down these thoughts and become aware of what you are thinking, you can literally begin to change your life.

Each thought holds its own energy-field. Yes, indeed, we do mean this literally. As each thought holds its own energy, you draw to you, the energy of that thought and thus create your reality. Please do not misunderstand, there may be a lapse or waiting period before it is manifested literally into your life. However, make no mistake; the power of the thought holds incredible potential or 'seed' to grow a life form. Yes, indeed, energy can do all of that and does it all the time.

As this book is being written the misuse of the mind has become a potential lethal weapon, so to speak. The negativity that fills most people's thoughts on a regular basis is filling the literal air-waves or atmosphere, if you will, with negative energy thought-forms as explained previously. The real challenge lies within getting your attention in such a way, that you realize the importance of taming the mind. When you are over-wrought and filled to the limit with over-thinking it is difficult to make you realize the incredible importance and all-encompassing power the thought-process has.

If you take the time to look in on your thoughts and begin the filtering process, you will begin to see a new life take form in front of your very eyes. It takes great courage to change a life-long habit; however we assure you it can be done! The very essence of a clear mind creates in its path, a directed, clear, and tranquil life so very missed by the masses at this time.

The other option lies in misuse of the mind and confusing the thought process. This is done by entertaining too many thoughts and allowing them to rule the roost. There is much work to be done; the sooner you get started on this project, the sooner you will see the tangible results in your life. Now, for the review thus far:

1) Give yourself permission to be a positive-thinker without fear, worry and indecision.
2) Know that by filtering your thoughts, you are creating a new and better reality for yourself.

Know your mind on a regular basis; what is in there? What stays, what goes?

Realize that when you take the time to clear you excess thoughts, you are in fact empowering yourself to become someone new! Those old thoughts that continue to run around in your head, continue to bring to you what you have always gotten in your life. Begin to understand and respect the immense power that the thoughts hold. On all levels of your being, you are creating from moment to moment. Hold the vision for yourself, now that you are able to control and direct your thoughts. Begin to give this more consideration from day to day, and you will see the changes that you are looking for. We do realize that it can be a challenge to break the old habit. However, with a little concentration and a willingness to release the old thought processes, the changes have begun.

Now step aside for a moment so that you can have a good look at your life. Take assessment of those things that continuously bother, annoy, distract, worry, anger or bring you down in general. Whenever you choose to take the path of least resistance, you are foregoing your need to worry about it and allowing the best situation to unfold for you. You will be very entertained by how this process works, we assure you! But, it does take the work and courage.

This training was not given in your schools and seems too simple to be for real. We assure you wholeheartedly, it is for real and you can begin to use this simple process to change your entire life. We stress here that it does take a willingness to step out of your own way. You have become the masters of your own undoing, so to speak, by constantly tripping yourselves up. You see, the trick to the process is consistency. As with all things, as you consistently review how you are feeling/thinking and choose your thoughts wisely; you are in control and guiding the helm of the ship. The thoughts are like the storms of life dragging you this way and that. This has become a normal, acceptable way to live for the mass population.

Begin the training process one step at a time. Your mind will follow suit because it must. Once you have mastered the ability to clear out those unwanted thoughts, worries etc., you then have a clean slate to begin to work with. This clean slate is of immeasurable power to you. You may write on it whatever you wish. Imagine the slate being filled with a bunch of gibberish, this thought and that thought, without any real focus or intention. This can fill up your slate pretty quickly and take away from you the power of your controlled thought process. You will be tested at every turn by outside events, people, concerns etc. in your ability to keep your slate clean.

Every time you choose the path of least resistance and clear your slate once again, you become the master of your own life. You will find it to be quite enjoyable once you get the hang of it. Without the need to 'do anything about it' frees you up to begin to become the master creator of your life. Self-judgment is another to be on the lookout for, for it can sap your energy and positive feelings about yourself very quickly. Self-judgment is almost encouraged by your society and is seen as an acceptable pastime. Have the courage dear ones to step aside. It only takes a moment of your time to do so every now and again. Your willingness and your choice in every moment to choose the positive will be the changing factor in your life.

The answer or solution will flow to you when you need it the most, when you turn off the 'worry machine', your mind chatter-box. You see, you have been operating in this manner for so long now, that it will take some doing to unplug it! Trust is the key for this process. In the beginning, the trusting will be a blind one, as you have not seen the results of this process first hand. However, once you have had your first experience with it, you will see that your world has not fallen apart and you are still alive! Most fears are unwarranted, have no true substance or origin, and only serve to keep you from achieving your goals and desires.

There will come a time in your near future where this ability to control the thought process will be a necessity, not a luxury. What we mean by this is that on the whole, humanity is advancing to a higher state of being. In this higher state, it becomes more and more necessary to be responsible for what you create for yourself. Simply adjust your thoughts so that it includes only what you desire to create, and not focusing on what you don't want.

By being the creator, you put yourself in a position of power and authority over your life. A simple adjustment is all it takes.

When you think of a television screen and the picture is out of focus, so it is with your mind. The excess thoughts keep your life 'out of focus.' This level of unclarity will bring you a jumble of events and situations that you do not necessarily want. Depending on your level of positive or negative, is what you will bring forward as your life experience. As you adjust your inner screen (your mind), to one of clarity and focus, so too will your life follow suit. It is just that simple. The level or degree, to which you can control your thoughts, will be the deciding factor for your ability to create the changes that you would like.

Realize that by utilizing your mind (in the correct way), you can have whatever it is that you desire. There are no limits, except in your imagination. Begin using all of the tools God gave you: your positive feelings, emotions, thoughts, visualization and imagination to create what you want. Intend and begin to draw to you your dreams. Energy is the key. As all thoughts are energy, as you focus upon what you want (not what you do not want) you begin to draw that very thing to you in a very real way. The time period that it takes to manifest into physical form is in direct relation to how much effort, concentration and desire you put forth into the atmosphere. It is a simple process, but one not used very often by most.

Accept the fact that you are responsible for all you create, and it is time to create what you truly want now! Why wait on such a gold-mine of opportunity? Know that by going within and working with the subconscious mind, you can release unwanted programming from childhood, institutions, society etc. Then you can begin reprogramming yourself, to such a degree, that you will see massive change taking place in all areas of your life. You see, the mind can expand very nicely once it has room to grow. Useless and negative thoughts cause the mind to shrink in fear, of usually unwarranted issues that truly need have no bearing over your life!

Why not then, begin the process today: release your fear, anger, self-hatred, judgment, worry, indecision and let loose the power of the mind! It's time to proceed and move forward. Use the capabilities given you and begin your project of self-creation. It will be quite an enlightening experience. Stop looking to others to show you the route. For when you quiet the mind, the path will be shown to you!

The tools and exercises contained in this book are to be used for your empowerment and freedom; helping you to create the life you were meant to live. By living in your power, and using your mind as the powerful tool that it was meant to be, you are free to create whatever you choose!

THE HEART KNOWS

"Apply your Intuitive knowing to everything you do. Let your heart be the ultimate guide when making decisions for yourself."

-Annett's Guides

◆ CHAPTER 13 ◆

BEING MENTALLY RESPONSIBLE

Please take into consideration the fact that your idea of what is considered normal in your day to day living, really is not. This way of being totally out of control and the mind being pulled this way and that is definitely not a normal thing! We do so wish that we could impress upon you the idea that you are infinitely powerful beings with a job to do. We mean here a job that is apart from your everyday bread and butter type. The other job that we speak of here is the one where you transform your life and that of those around you. Know that there is a higher path and another way to live. This has been hidden from you for some time, so to speak. The key here of course, once again, is to access the 'hidden' power of the mind.

As you so choose to be in control of your mind and not the other way around, it can do your bidding quite nicely, indeed! This tool, the mind needs taming on a regular basis. It can be a double-edged sword, you see. If you use it in the wrong way, it can cut you apart. When used properly, it is then a tool that serves you. Please never give up on this goal of clearing the mind. Now put another way, when you have built up a lifetime of negative thought-thinking, then it will take quite an effort on your part to change this habit. That is all it truly is, a habit – and one that you can change for yourself.

The time for this is NOW and in fact, probably 'yesterday'. There is much work to be done in this sphere of existence and you all have the ability to do it. By your choice you alone can begin to make a difference. You see, as one person awakens to their innate wisdom and power, they create a pathway for others to follow. This pathway is inhabited by the minority of Earth's people at present, however, with each new soul that crosses over to a new way of thinking and living, brings hope and a new awareness for the others. Stop for a moment and think of what a monumental gift you can give another: you as another link in the chain of positivity and light - can begin to help build a new world. We do not mean this lightly, we mean this literally. As a new awareness begins to develop among the people, action can then begin to be taken to connect with your own Divine Power and purpose.

Do you sometimes wonder why you are here, "What is my purpose for living?" Well, we say to you: be brave enough to look within yourself and you will begin to see a picture forming. At the present most are attempting to fill up from the outside in (materially). Although this is required of you to a degree, we also wish to point out that perhaps you have all gotten a little carried away and forgotten who you really are! Who you really are is connected to your inner- self; the only way to reach this self is to go within.

For most of you this is a terrifying prospect. When you are filled with over-thinking and busyness continuously it can be frightening to stop and take a look inside of yourself. Now that we have gotten your attention once again we can proceed to tell you how to go about this. At every turn, so to speak, you have the opportunity to listen to your inner-self. We mean that the highest part of yourself, your innate wisdom, is ready to speak to you at any given time if only you will listen to it. Be aware that by letting go a little bit more and trusting your inner guidance you are then on the path to self-discovery.

This goal is well worth your time we assure you. It may not be a familiar path but it is a much more worthwhile one. Come to know your true self or identity by connecting within on a regular basis. There is no other way to get to where you are going than this. Filling up from the outside in only serves to satisfy temporarily. The true nourishment of the soul must begin from the inside out. As you begin to become aware of your thoughts, you can begin to transform yourself and your life. Begin to open yourself up to the idea that this is possible, for indeed it is. It is your choice as to how much you choose to open up to this inner awareness and how much you choose to remain closed. Society on the whole has chosen to look the other way when it comes to inner awareness and responsibility for their actions. The general consensus is "We take what we need and let the next guy clean up the mess". Is this not true dear ones? It is indeed time for change. Only by beginning with inner awareness can this be possible. So then may we remind you once again to be mentally responsible for yourselves and not pick up any negativity along the way; yours or someone else's?

And so, please realize the power that you hold inside of yourselves, this power can multiply manifold when harnessed correctly. Once a soul begins to look for answers in a way that makes them 'stretch' from the inside, they have begun their journey. We would say to you: continue to search within for the answer; that is where the true power lies. Never give your power away to someone who says that they have all the answers at their disposal about YOU! Only you are the true authority on you. Many choose not to look at themselves very closely for fear of seeing who they really are, and that they might be disappointed. We can assure you, you will not. Once you begin to look within things begin to become much clearer and you then have many more options to choose from. If you choose to stay blind to who you really are you are, then you are 'cutting off your own arm', so to speak. This is a very limited perspective that most choose to see with. Once you begin to muster the courage to just BE with yourself in silence, the true work can begin.

May I now review what we have learned thus far: Firstly, start off the day with positive thoughts and the intention to stay connected to yourself in such a way as to know what you are thinking at all times. (NOT going on automatic pilot!). Secondly, to trust and then follow your intuition so as to begin to create the life you truly want. Thirdly, keep an open mind about how you will accomplish number one and two. An open mind is required dear ones, as this is when the knowledge can flow to you. If you are closed and rigid about life, it will be closed and rigid right back. Life always mirrors back to you what you choose to create in your life. There has been much come to pass over the years and we hope that this will open the minds of many.

You have a task at hand and it is one of urgency. Eventually your luck will run out and you will need to become responsible for yourselves in a way that you have not been before. This continuous mind chatter is a form of irresponsibility. If you cannot have peace in your mind then how will you achieve it in your outer manifestations, (your world?) And, some of you may say to this: that is ridiculous, the two have nothing to do with one another, and we say to you OH YES IT DOES! It has everything to do with it. As you think, so shall you create.

The time is coming very soon indeed where the rules of the game will change: those of you who are willing to look within and be responsible for yourselves, will excel in the game called life. Those who do not will see themselves being called on it without question. And the dice will be rolled: who is willing to play the game of life by the new rules, and who will stay with the old? For you see, in the times to come, there will no longer be a choice to be spiritually immature by continuing to do what you have always done, regardless if it is harmful to others or not. In this new life you will be held accountable for all you do and say and think and feel. So, let it be positive!

These words are not to scare you, they are meant simply as a wakeup call to your future. You will begin to see taking shape before your very eyes, a new way of existing in this reality. Please, also begin to release your fears, they merely hold you back from your own greatness and ability to manifest to your heart's content. These fears are mostly unfounded and if you were to look them squarely in the eye, you would see they no longer hold any power or control over you.

Now is the time dear ones, live in the moment, release your fears and love one another. Long ago someone was sent to teach you this lesson 'love thy neighbor as thyself', and how quickly it was forgotten by many. Please understand, your time truly is NOW, in fact it is long overdue. If you take a look at what state the world is in at present, you will know that something has gone terribly wrong and needs to be changed right now!

Allow me to demonstrate my point more fully: imagine a playground with children in a sandbox. They have not learned how to play nice and continue to fight and take from one another. Eventually someone more mature, a guardian of these young ones, will step in and put an end to the squabbling. In time someone will get hurt and the children will not have learned how to share and exist together in harmony. And so it is with the children of the Earth. They too, in their immaturity, continue to harm one another and fight amongst themselves in the name of power, greed and control of the lands. (Of which belongs to no one, and is meant to be shared equally among you). Are we beginning to make ourselves clear on this issue?

Much time has passed and it is expected that the children of earth would begin to grow up and become more spiritually responsible for themselves. Thus far, we have not seen too great a change, and can only hope that more of you will choose to participate in the Grand Master Plan. This plan is open for all to participate, who so choose. This plan includes a shifting to a higher level of being or consciousness that enables the earth to move to a higher level. There have also been those who choose to go within and support the Grand Master Plan for the earth and its people. Were it not for these in the minority, the earth would have been finished long ago! We are no longer playing a game of give and take here. The game has now become serious in its very nature and requires much more give on all your parts.

There will be so much more expected of each of you in the next years to follow. There will no longer be room for 'mistakes' such as prejudice, hatred, control, greed etc. These mistakes, dear children have now become fatal in what it is doing to the Earth and the energy she resonates with. If you choose to fight Mother Earth, we can tell you who will win and it will not be the children! Please begin to reach inside and find (perhaps remember) who you truly are in the big scheme of things. There has been much taken in the way of memory and knowledge from the children of the Earth. It is time to wake up and remember!

This book is as much a teaching tool as it is a wakeup call for all who will listen and pay attention to the emergency situation that it has become. If you continue to create hatred, distrust, war and disharmony then eventually you will be held accountable for your actions, yes? This topic is a very heavy one and we understand it creates fear in some of you, however, please be reminded; what affects the one affects the many. We are truly all one and are connected at the heart level. If you choose to hurt another, you hurt yourself also. And if you do not see the results of your actions right away, then eventually it will catch up to you.

There are no injustices on a karmic level, all is accounted for. Please spread love and light by which to see; this is beneficial not only to yourself, but to all. The energy of love is so very powerful that it has the ability to transform all in its path immediately. By use of this energy called love, you will eventually transform the Earth into the Eden it was meant to be before the dark forces began to join in the game. That is all fine and dandy, for all are learning experiences and lessons. However, it is time to play a different hand and begin to transform the Earth. This transformation will take place with or without you. We do sincerely wish it will be with you. The next several years bring incredible opportunity to the student of life who is willing to play by the new rules. For them a door will be opened and a new life will be born out of love.

Please begin to shift your thinking to a higher level; one of peace, joy, love and harmony with your fellow human beings. We trust that this can be done and look forward to watching you transform yourselves and your Earth. Peace has been waiting for a very, very long time to reign once more. And so it shall. When the clock runs out, those who continue on in their harmful ways will exit the picture and make way for those with love in their hearts.

SELF HEALING

"Look and feel with your inner eyes and you will see your inner self shining through. Trust that relaxation and repairing of the body is okay, release self-destruct, self-harshness. Know you are well. Trust

& allow the body to open its pathways to healing. Adjust your body by asking it to come into balance: ask it to let go of all negativity and keep itself in check! It will do your bidding quite nicely if you ask."

-Annett's Guides

WHAT KUTHUMI MEANS TO ME

The Master Kuthumi represents a higher version of me. When I follow the guidance that I receive from within, I connect with my own Inner Master. Those who have gone before us, have mastered their lives and moved on to a higher state of consciousness, are pointing the way for us to follow. To become masters of our own lives, we must learn from someone who has gone before us.

In this way, we can begin to realize the highest potential for ourselves. To master the mind, is the gift that Kuthumi offers us in this book. Without this guidance and understanding, I don't think I would be where I am today! I chose to be the navigator and creator of my life, and therefore the right tools appeared. We can all do and be what Kuthumi has aspired to, with focus and effort on our part. Kuthumi teaches self-mastery, self-responsibility and focused awareness. The end result is freedom from mind chatter and the ability to create what you want in your life!

TOOLS FOR SELF-EMPOWERMENT

Below are techniques I have used for myself and clients, to clear negative patterns and change beliefs to begin the self-healing process. They can assist you to achieve your goals and live an empowered life.

SELF-HYPNOSIS

Anyone can use self-hypnosis. It is simply a different brain-wave, a very relaxed state of being where we can access your subconscious mind. This is the place where all changes are made that can help you move forward in life!

The answers are all inside of you. Your subconscious mind stores all memories, experiences & traumas. Your cells have memory and store them permanently until they are cleared & replaced with a positive emotion (such as self-acceptance/self-love).

A similar state to meditation, but uses specific techniques to create the changes you want. Healing through hypnosis, you are able to get to the root source of the problem.

The changes are done on all levels, spiritual, emotional, mental and physical. Your brain is like a computer; we can remove negative, out-dated files and replace them with positive ones.

Many of us are still operating on an unwanted belief we learned from when we were five! When you are ready for change and to move forward, hypnotherapy is a most powerful tool.

Using a technique called Parts Therapy we can discover the part inside of you causing the problem. This technique has been highly successful for myself and many others.

Some areas that Hypnotherapy has successfully helped are:

Weight loss, addictions, sleeping, relaxation, health/healing, changing negative beliefs, past lives, confidence etc.

REIKI

Reiki is an energy that can best be described as love. It balances your system and activates the body's innate ability to heal itself. The energy is transmitted through the hands and clears the mind, preparing the body to self-heal. The client remains fully clothed and the energy is transmitted through a gentle touch. **Reiki Level 1, 2 and Master classes available. Benefits include:**

Decreases stress, enhances sleep, eliminates pain, improves overall well-being, and removes energy blockages. It aligns the energy of your mental, emotional, physical and spiritual bodies. The reiki attunement (through reiki training) can help you find your life's purpose.

PSYCHOLOGICAL KINESIOLOGY (Psych-K©)

Your subconscious mind has all the answers you need. With this method, you communicate with your subconscious mind through kinesiology (muscle testing). Your electrical circuitry of the body will be strong and hold for a yes/truth and will be weak for a no for you.

You are able to remove negative beliefs/blocks and reprogram your mind to hold a positive belief. You can also program for a specific goal or work with an issue you wish to clear.

If you are sabotaging" yourself because of fear of success or failure, we will remove that and replace it with a self-supporting belief.

Some of the changes I have seen for myself and clients:

- **Pain relief**
- **Cleared claustrophobia**
- **Hormone balance (cleared hot flashes)**
- **Confidence**

Note: you can also personally ask Angels & your spirit guides for help in any area of your life and you will receive it! Just ask in your mind and assistance will come in a way that is for your highest good at that specific time in your life. Then pay attention to the guidance that comes.

RETREATS

- Quantum Healing Activation Technique QHAT Certification retreats.
- Life Transformed Level I and Level II training.
- Reiki and Quantum Relaxation retreats for healers.

QUANTUM HEALING

Using heart frequency to clear the energy pattern in the cell causing the imbalance . Connecting to the consciousness and innate wisdom of the body to heal itself.

I was so grateful to have the connection to quantum healing that I was inspired to create an 8 week Quantum Healing Activation Technique Program for practitioners.

8 week Q.H.A.T. Program
Quantum Healing Activation Technique Training

This course is an experiential transformational training that will help you become more of your authentic self; a transition from your old identity to the true you.

- Experience physical and emotional pain relief
- Working with sending and receiving heart frequency quantum energy
- Receiving chakra clearing and activations to easier access the energy.
- How to protect your energy field and stay balanced when working with others.
- How to communicate with your higher self via self muscle testing
- How to connect with the sacred heart to access high frequency that can create what would be considered "miracle healing"
- How to see, feel and connect to the consciousness of the body and run frequency that lets the body begin to heal itself physically and emotionally.
- Work with other students in a group to practice giving and receiving quantum heart frequency share healing, creating friendship and community.
- Connect to the intelligence of your own organs and systems in your body
- Receive powerful messages about your life and health
- 8 live training classes plus 8 recorded training modules
- Receive healing in every module as you work through the program.
- Move bones into place and strengthen your clairaudient, clairsentient and clairvoyant abilities

"I was so intrigued with the quantum heart frequency that helped me release the sugar addiction that I signed up for your 8 week course. Wow! Love love love that too!!! I also love that you give me opportunity to practice running the frequency on you and get feedback. I look forward to taking more one on one sessions and classes in the future! You are such a God send!" -Cathy from Alaska.

Group Coaching

Quantum Healing Transformation Program for Pain Relief and Health:

- Live weekly group healing, transformation & coaching
- Physical and emotional pain relief
- Releasing your old identity and transform into your true self
- Raising your frequency
- Get your freedom back to live your soul's purpose
- Get answers about YOUR life and make the shift!
- Transform in a group with others

Learn how to see, feel and connect to the consciousness of the body, be aware of what is happening and run frequency that lets the body begin to heal itself physically and emotionally.

How to heal chronic fatigue syndrome, sugar addiction, candida and other chronic illnesses by finding the root cause so the body can heal itself.

Shows how peace of mind leads to literally creating a better reality for us all; one that is free of destruction, chaos, negativity and fear. Teaches how to clean up our thought pollution and create a new Earth. Peace on Earth first begins with peace of mind.

"Love yourself first and you will find the love you are seeking from another. There is no need to play the repetition game over and over again. Step out of the cycle of self-sabotage and see that you have what it takes to know who you really are. Never settle for less and it will no longer be a part of your reality." -Kuthumi

Are You Ready For Our New Earth?

Peace be with you. Accept yourself as you are to begin with. Then, decide what you will change for the better and begin to visualize your new life as you would have it be. If you cannot get a clear picture of how it will manifest into form, simply begin to give this thought-form 'life' by energizing it with your positive thoughts about it. Thus, your creating has begun.

Know that in your heart, lies the real you, regardless of what was 'done to you'. This realization alone can help you transform yourself back to wholeness. Understand, dear one that you were brought to this experience in order to learn and to grow, not to be punished.

The idea is to accept the fact that you participated in this event in your life in order to learn about a facet of yourself. The goal is to become bigger than you are now. Don't be concerned with how it affected you; be more concerned with how the event changed you for the better. See how it expanded your awareness of who you really are! That is the key to self growth. *-Kuthumi*

*Inside flap of book (or other promotional area):

Are You In Control Of Your Thoughts

Or Are They In Control Of You?

After being attuned to reiki in 1998 Annett had a spiritual awakening, opening a channel to communicate with guides, angels and masters. It was her wake up call to life. This is your wakeup call!

- Learn how to use heart frequency to heal yourself
- A self-help tool for pain relief & healing chronic illness
- Connect to your power & guidance within
- Learn control of the mind; your personal power source
- Includes practical, easy-to-use exercises that anyone can learn

About The Author

In 1998 after being attuned to Reiki, Annett had a visitation by an Angel and began to connect with Guides, Angels and Ascended Masters.

After asking "What can I do to help fulfill my soul's purpose?"

Her Guide answered: "Gather groups, assist to guide them to their soul's purpose and help activate their light within"...

Annett has had a successful healing business since 1998. She has a Psychology/Sociology education, is a Quantum energy healer, Creator of Quantum Healing Activation Technique (Q.H.A.T) Certification Program, Reiki Master, Hypnotherapist and transformation coach.

Working with clearing trauma from the cell memory, Annett has helped many people heal themselves and transform their lives. It is said that reiki puts you on your life's path. Many doors have opened for her since she has begun to walk the spiritual path and listen to the voice of the Higher Self. She loves teaching students how to use quantum energy to transform themselves and their lives.

Some of her hobbies are sound healing with hang drum, meditation, yoga, and playing classical guitar. She lives in Victoria, BC and enjoys the independence of teaching, writing, traveling, and gathering spiritual community through retreats.

www.annettschneider.com
schneider_annett@hotmail.com

Quantum healing for people and pets meetup

Made in the USA
Columbia, SC
07 January 2020